JESUS AND PAUL
Parallel Lives

Jerome Murphy-O'Connor, O.P.

A Michael Glazier Book

LITURGICAL PRESS
Collegeville, Minnesota

www.litpress.org

A Michael Glazier book published by Liturgical Press

Cover design by David Manahan, o.s.b. Illustrations: El Greco, Christ Redeemer and Saint Paul the Apostle; both from the Casa y Museo del Greco, Toledo, Spain. Credit: Erich Lessing/Art Resource, New York.

1   2   3   4   5   6   7   8   9

Library of Congress Cataloging-in-Publication Data

Murphy-O'Connor, J. (Jerome), 1935–
    Jesus and Paul : parallel lives / Jerome Murphy-O'Connor.
        p. cm.
    "A Michael Glazier book."
    Includes bibliographical references.
    ISBN-13: 978-0-8146-5173-5
    ISBN-10: 0-8146-5173-9
    1. Jesus Christ—Biography.   2. Paul, the Apostle, Saint.   I. Title.

BT301.3.M87 2007
232.9'01—dc22
[B]   2006030167

To K. Ashe

for forty-eight years of friendship

Contents

Abbreviations

AJ   Josephus, *The Antiquities of the Jews.*

BAGD   W. Bauer, W. F. Arntd, F. W. Gingrich, and F. W. Danker, *A Greek-English Lexicon of the New Testament and Other Early Christian Literature.* 2nd ed. Chicago: University of Chicago Press, 1979.

JW   Josephus, *The Jewish War.*

m.   *The Mishnah*, translated by H. Danby, Oxford, Oxford University Press, 1933.

OCD   *The Oxford Classical Dictionary.* Third edition edited by S. Hornblower and A. Spawforth, Oxford, Oxford University Press, 1996.

PL   J. Migne, *Patrologia latina.*

TU   Texte und Untersuchungen.

Preface

While I owe the subtitle to Plutarch, this little book makes no attempt to emulate his famous series of *Parallel Lives*. Plutarch (ca. 50–ca. 120 C.E.) was one of the most prolific and influential authors of antiquity. Though he traveled widely, he retained his birthplace, Chaeroneia, as his permanent base, even though it had no great library and lacked the intellectual equals who could provide learned discussion. His reason reveals the best side of Plutarch: "I live in a little town, and it pleases me to stay there lest it grow even smaller" (*Life of Demosthenes* 2.2). Such sly humor hints at the quality of insight that made him a great biographer. The *Parallel Lives* are twenty-three volumes, each containing a pair of biographies, first that of an eminent Greek statesman followed by that of a Roman who is in some way comparable; in four, the Roman appears first. Alexander the Great, for example, is paired with Julius Caesar. In each the focus is on character *(êthos)* as it is revealed and molded by political action. Thus, Plutarch says with great perception,

> the most outstanding exploits do not always have the property of revealing the goodness or badness of the agent; often in fact, a casual action, the odd phrase, or a jest reveals character better than battles involving the loss of thousands upon thousands of lives . . . just as a painter reproduces his subject's likeness by concentrating on the face and the expression of the eyes, by means of which character is revealed, and pays hardly any attention to the rest of the body. (*Life of Alexander* 1; trans. Waterfield)[1]

Despite this disclaimer Plutarch does not offer snippets but rather complete life-histories. He begins with the family into which the subject is born, then deals with the intellectual and moral influences that formed the character, and treats the victories and failures, the turning points and crises through which the hero lived.

I have attempted this sort of biography for Paul in *Paul: His Story*, but it is manifestly impossible in the case of Jesus. Plutarch, however, justifies my focus on a series of coincidences in the lives of Jesus and Paul. Not only were Jesus and Paul born within a year or so of each other, but as children they suffered the traumatic experience of being forced into exile with their parents. In that new and very different environment they were molded by forces that led them to confront questions that they probably never would have faced had they not been refugees. As young men they freely chose lifestyles that demanded complete obedience to the Law of Moses. Yet at a certain point they both realized that they had made the wrong decision. As a result they rejected the Law completely. Finally both died at the hands of the Romans.

To compare and contrast Jesus and Paul in terms of these events reveals aspects of their personalities and circumstances that have not received the attention they deserve.[2]

Jerusalem   Jerome Murphy-O'Connor, o.p.

9 October 2006

---

[1] Plutarch, *The Greek Lives. A Selection of Nine Greek Lives,* trans. R. Waterfield (Oxford: Oxford University Press, 1998) 312.

[2] A note about Scripture translation in this book: I generally rely on the Revised Standard Version of Scripture but often make my own translation when necessary.

Chapter 1

The Same Age

It is often thought that Jesus and Paul represent different generations. Jesus is seen as the symbol of a Palestinian Aramaic-speaking church, which some ten or so years later gave birth to a Greco-Roman Greek-speaking church best represented by Paul, a diaspora Jew from Tarsus in Cilicia. In fact Jesus and Paul were approximately the same age. Absolute precision is impossible, but there is a real convergence.

Jesus

The New Testament offers two accounts of the birth and childhood of Jesus. Even if we leave the details aside, the structures of the two narratives are not only different but contradictory.

For Matthew 1–2, Mary and Joseph are natives of Bethlehem, where Jesus was born. Fear of Herod the Great forced them first to flee to Egypt, and then fear of his son, Archelaus, obliged them to substitute Nazareth for Bethlehem as their new permanent residence.

For Luke 1–2, on the contrary, Mary and Joseph are natives of Nazareth. At a very awkward moment for Mary who is close to term, they were forced to travel to Bethlehem because a census had been ordered by the emperor Augustus. After the birth of Jesus in Bethlehem, they make a visit to the Temple in Jerusalem, and then return to Nazareth.

The incompatibility of the two accounts means we are confronted by independent sources with radically different visions of what went on "in the days of Herod the king" (Matt 2:1; Luke 1:5). One does not depend on the other. Hence, what they have in common is important, because one confirms the other. As regards the structure, however, a choice must be made. Both cannot be correct.

The linchpin of Luke's narrative is the census. Without it there would be no journey from Nazareth and no birth in Bethlehem. Is what Luke tells us about this event historically reliable? The majority of scholars will answer in the negative. According to Luke, (1) the census was ordered by the emperor Augustus; (2) it was conducted by Quirinius the governor of the Roman province of Syria; and (3) the key regulation was that males had to return to their father's house to be counted (Luke 2:1-5). Each of these elements is problematic.[1]

(1) There is no evidence of a general imperial census in the reign of Augustus. Had there been such a census, it would not have been applicable to Palestine, which was an independent kingdom ruled by Herod the Great and associated with Rome but not part of the Empire. (2) There was a Roman official called Quirinius, and he did supervise a census in Palestine, but this took place in 6 C.E. when Rome dismissed Herod's son, Archelaus, after a reign of ten years, and assumed direct control of Judea and Samaria. This, however, would be the year when Jesus made his visit to the Temple at the age of twelve (Luke 2:41-42), long after his birth. (3) No Roman census regulation required a person to travel far. Registration took place in the place where one lived or, if that was too small, at the chief town of the taxation district. Moreover, wives and children were not required to appear in person. The head of the family answered for them.

Matthew's Narrative

If the linchpin of the census is removed, Luke's artificial framework disappears. His narrative falls apart into its component elements, whose individual historicity is another matter. Thus the only framework of the childhood of Jesus is that of Matthew. What he tells us is internally consistent, but cannot be taken at face value as an eyewitness account of what actually occurred. His narrative is carefully structured in order to serve as a prologue to the Gospel, telling the reader in chapter 1 *who* Jesus is, "He shall be called Emmanuel" (Matt 1:23) and in chapter 2 *whence* he comes, "He shall be called a Nazorean" (Matt 2:23).

Matthew 2 is a highly sophisticated document of which the greater part is due to Matthew's creativity. He had two sources: (1) the Magi Story, and (2) the Flight and Return Story, both of which he accepted as historical. They recounted events in the childhood of Jesus that he believed actually happened. Matthew felt it was his right as a storyteller not merely to retell what had been passed on to him but to make it more attractive and to give it greater impact by filling out the picture. Thus on the basis of the brief note "Herod is about to seek the child to kill him" Matthew developed the dramatic conspiracy story of Matthew 2:1-12, and the massacre of the children of Bethlehem.

The Magi Story

(1) When Jesus was born in Bethlehem of Judah in the days of Herod the king, wise men *(magoi)* from the east came, (9b) and the star which they had seen in its rising went before them, till coming it stood over the place where the child *(paidion)* lay. (11) And going into the house they saw the child *(paidion)* with Mary his mother, and falling they worshiped him. Then opening their treasures, they offered him gifts, gold and frankincense and myrrh. (12) Then they departed to their own country.

The Flight and Return

(13b) Behold, an angel of the Lord appeared in a dream to Joseph saying, "Rise, take the child *(paidion)* and his mother, and flee into Egypt, and remain there until I speak to you, for Herod is about to seek the child to kill him." (14) Rising, he took the child *(paidion)* and his mother by night and departed into Egypt. (15) And he was there until the death of Herod [when] (19b) behold, an angel of the Lord appeared in a dream to Joseph (20) saying, "Rise, take the child *(paidion)* and his mother, and go into the land of Israel, for those seeking the life of the child *(paidion)* have died." (21) Rising, he took the child *(paidion)* and his mother and entered the land of Israel.

I do not believe the Magi Story is historical, but evidence wll be furnished in the next chapter that the substance of the Flight and Return Story actually happened. Here, however, we are concerned with only one aspect, namely, the light they throw on the date of the birth of Jesus. In both Jesus is called a *paidion*. In the Flight-Return source he is a *paidion* both before and after the death of Herod the Great that occurred shortly before Passover in 4 B.C.E., which that year fell on 11 April.[2] Luke also regularly describes Jesus as a *paidion* (1:59, 66, 76, 80; 2:17, 27, 40). Hence, the fundamental question is: what exactly does *paidion* mean?

The standard translations (RSV, NRSV, NJB, NAB) all render *paidion* by "child," but this is a polyvalent term whose value changes according to the way it is used. To say that "X is the child of Y" tells us nothing of the age of X. Similarly "the children of God" (Heb 2:13) can be of any age. Those whom Jesus affectionately addressed as "children" in John 21:5 were adult fishermen. When age, rather than relationship, is specifically in question, *paidion* is the diminutive of *pais*, "boy, youth" (which is used of the twelve-year-old Jesus in Luke 2:43), and specifically means "a very young child, an infant" without any connotation of gender (BAGD, 604).

Clearly *paidion* can be applied to a newborn child (John 16:21), and to a three-month-old baby (AJ 2.218), but what is the upper limit of its application? In other words, how old does a child have to be for *paidion* to be inappropriate? Philo quotes Pseudo-Hippocrates, who said,

> In the nature of man there are seven seasons, which men call ages: infancy, childhood, boyhood and the rest:
>
> He is an infant [*paidion*] until he reaches his seventh year, the age of the shedding of his teeth. He is a child [*pais*] until he arrives at the age of puberty, which takes place in fourteen years. (*De opifico mundi* 105; trans. Yonge)[3]

Philo approvingly also quotes Solon, the Athenian lawgiver (635–560 B.C.E.) to the effect that the first period of a child's life lasts seven years (*De opifico mundi* 104). Similarly Shakespeare, for whom schooling began when an infant was seven years old,

> All the world's a stage,
> And all the men and women merely players:
> They have their exits and their entrances;
> And one man in his time plays many parts,
> His acts being seven ages. As, first the infant,
> Mewing and puking in the nurse's arms.
> And then the whining schoolboy, with his satchel
> And shining morning face, creeping like a snail
> Unwillingly to school. (*As You Like It*, II, 7)

Such consistency over such a long period in such varied sources betrays a commonsense observation that a significant change takes place in a child's seventh year. In the Catholic Church, for example, it is thought to be the age when a child becomes morally responsible (cf. 1 Cor 14:21).

Having established that in antiquity a child could be called a *paidion* from birth to the age of seven, we now come to the next question: is it possible to narrow down this figure? In other words, what did the evangelists think that *paidion* meant relative to Jesus?

Apropos of John the Baptist Luke wrote, "On the eighth day they came to circumcise the child *(paidion)*" (1:59). And with respect to the shepherds, "They went with haste and found Mary and Joseph and the babe *(brephos)* lying in a manger. And when they saw it they made known the saying which had been told them concerning this child *(peri tou paidiou toutou)*" (2:16-17). John is eight days old, and Jesus even younger, a newborn. Unfortunately, the only reference to an absolute date that Luke gives us is the census (2:1), which we have seen to be completely unreliable.

Matthew is more helpful. His Flight-Return source presents Jesus as a *paidion* both before (2:13) and after the death of Herod the Great (2:20). The story of the massacre of the innocents (2:16-18) is entirely a Matthean creation (see chapter 2). It was developed to underline graphically the danger to Jesus, and the way it is described is highly significant. "Herod sent and killed all the children *(pantas tous paidas)* . . . who were two years old and younger" (2:16). This suggests that for Matthew any child over two was a *pais*, whereas any child under two was a *paidion*. In other words, within the seven-year span covered by *paidion*, Matthew made the commonsense distinction between a child who has to be carried and one that can walk. By the age of two most children are fully mobile.

This distinction was one of the bones of contention between the Pharisaic schools of the strict Shammai and the more liberal Hillel. A "child" was not obligated to make the Passover pilgrimage. Hence the question,

> Who is deemed a child? Any that cannot ride on his father's shoulders and go up from Jerusalem to the Temple Mount. So the School of Shammai. And the School of Hillel says: Any that cannot hold his father's hand and go up [on his feet] from the Jerusalem to the Temple Mount. *(m. Hagigah* 1.1; trans. Danby)[4]

All that can be said, however, is that Matthew understood the Jesus of his source to be a babe in arms at the time of Herod's death. It would be going too far to say that this assessment was rooted in a historical recollection of the real age of Jesus.[5] While this is not impossible, it is not demanded by the evidence.

In another redactional passage Matthew makes the wise men ask "where is he who has been born the king of the Jews?" (2:2). It is possible to see "the king of the Jews" as standing in apposition to "he who has been born," but commonsense demands that "he who has been born" be understood as attributive, i.e., to function effectively as an adjective.

Hence, one should translate "where is the newborn king of the Jews"[6] or "where is the infant king of the Jews" (NJB against NRSV). Once again Matthew shows his understanding of *paidion*, but this time in his Magi source. The child was born not long before the wise men sought him.

In conclusion, all that can be said is that Matthew was convinced that Jesus was born in the two years or so preceding the death of Herod that occurred shortly before Passover in 4 B.C.E. That year Passover fell on 11 April.

Paul

The only clue that Paul gives us to the date of his birth is to be found in Philemon 9 where he describes himself as a *presbytês* who is also a prisoner for Christ Jesus. The RSV and NAB translate this term as "ambassador," whereas the NRSV and NJB render it as "old man." The Greek word for "ambassador" is usually spelled *presbeutês*, but this term does not appear in any manuscript of Philemon. *Presbytês*, however, can mean an "ambassador." In 2 Maccabees 11:34 we read the beginning of a letter, "Quintus Memmius and Titus Manius, ambassadors of the Romans *(presbytai Rômaiôn)* to the people of the Jews, greetings." This appears to be the only certain attestation, but there are other passages whose scribes evidently thought the two terms to be interchangeable, e.g., LXX 2 Chronicles 32:31; 1 Maccabees 14:22; 15:17. The association is obvious. Ambassadors were always mature, dignified figures.

The only argument that can be invoked in favor of the meaning "ambassador" in Philemon 9 is the parallel in Ephesians 6:19-20 where Paul is presented as asking for prayers "that utterance be given me in opening my mouth boldly to proclaim the mystery of the gospel for which I am acting as an ambassador in chains *(hyper hou presbeuô en halysei)*." Not only is Ephesians not from the hand of Paul, but the circumstances of the two statements are different. In Ephesians it is a question of a proud boast, whereas in Philemon, Paul makes use of subtle moral blackmail in order to win Philemon's sympathy, "Not only am I an old man, but also a prisoner for Christ Jesus." There is little real doubt that *presbytês* in Philemon 9 must be taken as a reference to Paul's age.

But how old was "old"? What would Paul's contemporaries have understood by *presbytes*? The theoretical answer to this question is furnished by Philo, who can be fairly taken to represent the voice of antiquity, given the sources he uses. I begin with his second quote, from Pseudo-Hippocrates, because it uses *presbytes*.

He is a man *(anêr)* until he reaches his forty-ninth year, or seven times seven periods. He is an elderly man *(presbytês)* till he is fifty-six, eight times seven years old. And after that he is an old man *(gerôn)*. *(De opifico mundi* 105)[7]

Presbytes designates the second last stage of life. This highlights a problem of translation because if "old" is used for the second last age, the final age must be called something like "ancient." This is less than appropriate. Hence, *presbytes* in Philemon 9 should be rendered "elderly," which permits us to use "old" for the terminal period of life. "Elderly" we are told explicitly covers the years from fifty to fifty-six.

In the same context, however, Philo quotes another version of the ages of life, that of Solon of Athens (635–560 B.C.E.), which he himself adopts. Against the seven ages of Pseudo-Hippocrates, Solon divides life into ten ages of seven years. Of the last two ages he says,

When nine such periods have passed
His powers, though milder grown, still last;
When God has granted ten times seven,
The aged man prepares for heaven. *(De opifico mundi* 104; trans. Yonge)[8]

From the structure of Solon's text it is clear that the ninth age is from fifty-six to sixty-three, while the tenth age is from sixty-four to seventy. Philo takes over this structure and gives a personal twist to the interpretation,

In the ninth [age] his passions assume a mildness and gentleness from being to a great degree tamed. In the tenth [age] the desirable end of life comes upon him, while his limbs and organic senses are still unimpaired; for excessive old age is apt to weaken and enfeeble them all. *(De opifico mundi* 103; trans. Yonge 1993, 15)[9]

The underlying assumption both of Solon and of Philo is that the ideal span of life is seventy years. Solon said, "I set the limits of man's life at 70 years" (Herodotus, *Histories* 1.32). Philo would have certainly subscribed to the biblical view, "The days of our life are seventy years, or perhaps eighty, if we are strong" (Ps 90:10; *Jubilees* 23:15). Thus, given that the length of the individual stages was traditionally fixed at seven years, they had to produce ten stages to complete the schema. It is not difficult to detect an element of artificiality, compounded by the fact that neither gives a specific name to each stage.

When looked at from this perspective, the schema of Pseudo-Hippocrates is much more realistic. He too was constrained by the seven-year stage, but his development obviously reflects traditional terminology combined with medical insight. Note in particular that the prime of life (*aner* "man") is not divided into meaningless substages.

paidion	"infant"	0–7 years
pais	"child"	8–14
meirakion	"boy"	15–21
neaniskos	"youth"	22–28
aner	"man"	29–49
presbytes	"elderly"	50–56
geron	"old"	57–

Some confirmation of this approach is to be found in Judaism where a significant change takes place at the age of sixty. In terms of his redemption price, the value of a man dropped from fifty silver sanctuary shekels to fifteen shekels when he attained the age of sixty (Lev 27:2-7). Among the Essenes a judge had to retire at that age, and the justification given is that God willed that "man's understanding should decline before their days are fulfilled" (*Damascus Document* 10:7-10). Presumably this was also the reason why the priest who was overseer of the Many should retire at sixty (*Damascus Document* 14:6-7).

The conclusion to be drawn is that after a man had passed sixty he was considered to be "old," that is, in the last stage of life. Jerome, for example, consistently restricts "old" to people of sixty or over.[10] Thus, when Paul thought of himself as "elderly" he must have been approaching sixty. When one considers his lifestyle right up to his death, it is most improbable that Paul suffered from what Hippocrates considered the medical problems of old people (*Aphorisms* 3.36).

The most probable date for Philemon is the summer of 53 C.E.[11] If Paul was 58 or 59 when he wrote it, he would have been born in 6 or 5 B.C.E., approximately the date of the birth of Jesus.

Notes

[1] Emil Schürer, *The History of the Jewish People in the Age of Jesus Christ (175 BC–AD 135)* (Edinburgh: Clark, 1973–87) 1:399–427.

[2] Schürer, *The History of the Jewish People in the Age of Jesus Christ,* 1:327.

[3] C. D. Yonge, *The Works of Philo* (Peabody, MA: Hendrickson, 1993) 16.

[4] H. Danby, *The Mishnah* (Oxford: Oxford University Press, 1933) 211.

[5] See W. D. Davies, and Dale Allison, *A Critical and Exegetical Commentary on the Gospel of Matthew. I. Chs. 1–7*, International Critical Commentary (Edinburgh: Clark, 1988) 266, as against Raymond E. Brown, *The Birth of the Messiah. A Commentary on the Infancy Narratives in Matthew and Luke*, New Updated Edition (New York: Doubleday, 1993) 205, 228 n. 42.

[6] Brown, *The Birth of the Messiah*, 170; Davies and Allison, *A Critical and Exegetical Commentary on the Gospel of Matthew. I. Chs. 1–7*, 233; Ulrich Luz, *Das Evangelium nach Matthäus*, 1 Teilband, Mt 1–7, Evangelish-katholischer Kommentar zum Neuen Testament 1/1 (Zurich: Benziger/Neukirchen: Neukirchener Verlag, 1985) 112.

[7] Yonge, *The Works of Philo*, 16.

[8] Ibid., 15.

[9] Ibid., 15.

[10] J.N.D. Kelly, *Jerome. His Life, Writings, and Controversies* (London: Duckworth, 1975) 339.

[11] Jerome Murphy-O'Connor, *Paul. A Critical Life* (Oxford: Clarendon Press, 1996) 184.

Ripped from Their Roots: Child Refugees

The second parallel between Jesus and Paul is that both became refugees while still children. Too young to understand, they undoubtedly felt, however obscurely, the fear emanating from their parents as they faced a future of danger and uncertainty, far from the security of the familiar.

Jesus

One of the two sources that enabled Matthew to write chapter 2 of his Gospel is the story of the flight of Joseph and his family into Egypt and eventual return to Palestine. It reads:

> (13) Behold, an angel of the Lord appeared to Joseph in a dream, and said, "Rise, take the child and his mother, and flee to Egypt, and remain there till I tell you, for Herod is about to seek the child to kill him." (14) And he arose and took the child and his mother by night, and departed to Egypt, (15) and remained there until the death of Herod [when] (19) behold an angel appeared in a dream to Joseph saying, (20) "Rise take the child and his mother, and go to the land of Israel, for those who sought the child's life are dead." (21) And he rose and took the child and his mother and went into the land of Israel. (Matt 2:13-21)

This simple story contains no problems, but it does give rise to a question that is not often asked. Why was such an event ever remembered? Not only does it have no relationship to the ministry of Jesus, but he is too young to be an active agent. He does nothing. He is simply there as a mere appendage of his parents, who make decisions and take initiatives. Jesus' place is so far in the background that one is forced to wonder why the story was ever told about him.

Motive for Remembrance

There was one group in the early church, however, who had a vital interest in the story, namely, Jewish Christians. With great insight David Daube wrote:

> Imagine the Jews who adhered to Jesus celebrating the Passover in the years following the crucifixion. We know that they went on celebrating it fully since the Temple was not yet destroyed. As such a group—a family outside Jerusalem, a band of pilgrims in the city—assembled in the evening to dwell on the rescue from Egypt, the pattern of divine intervention and salvation, is it conceivable that they confined themselves to the customary tales, reflections and prayers, without introducing what was for them the fulfilment of it all. Surely not.[1]

The story of Jesus in Egypt offered Jewish Christians a supplemental way to Christianize Passover. Even though he was too young to have had any responsibility, Jesus had lived through a traumatic event that paralleled the experience of the Jewish people as symbolized by Jacob in the *Passover Haggadah*.[2] The points of contact between the two narratives are striking.

Flight and Return Story	**Passover Hagaddah**
1) *Danger* (v. 13d) Herod is about to seek the child to destroy him.	1) *Danger* (I, 1) The Aramean sought to destroy my Father.
2) *Divine Command* (v. 13b) Take the child and his mother and flee to Egypt.	2) *Divine Command* (II, 1) "And he went down to Egypt"; compelled by the word of God.
3) *Temporary Stay* (v. 13c) Remain there until I tell you	3) *Temporary Stay* (II, 2) He did not go down into Egypt to to settle there but only to sojourn.

4) *Return* (v. 20)	4) *Return* (VII, 1)
Take the child and his mother and go to the land of Israel.	"The Lord brought us forth from Egypt": Not by means of an angel, nor by means of a messenger, but the Holy One, blessed be He, Himself.

Jacob is threatened by Laban (I, 1), as Jesus was by Herod, but the move to Egypt is motivated by a divine command (II, 1). In both cases the sojourn in Egypt is intended to be temporary (II, 2), i.e., until the danger had passed. Equally the return from Egypt is the work of the Lord (VII, 1). The one difference between the two narratives is more apparent than real. The *Passover Haggadah* insists on the direct intervention of God (VII, 1), whereas Matthew employs the surrogate "an angel of the Lord" (v. 13a). At the time there were two schools of thought within Judaism regarding angels. There were those, such as Matthew, who saw them as a useful tool to protect divine transcendence. God did not act directly in history but by means of an agent. Others, however, such as the author of the *Passover Haggadah,* believed that powerful, intelligent, supernatural beings endangered monotheism.

Two further points of contact must be mentioned. First, Laban is identified as an Aramean, whereas Herod was an Idumean. In the square Hebrew consonantal script the difference is only one letter, *ʾrmy* "Aramean" versus *ʾdmy* "Idumean." Moreover, the shape of the two letters is almost the same, which facilitated a punning reference. They each have horizontal and vertical elements, but in *daleth* the junction is right-angled, whereas in *resh* it is curved. Second, both Laban and Herod were hated half-Jews.

Since it was the *Passover Haggadah* (among other material) that determined why Jesus' childhood sojourn in Egypt was retained in the popular memory, it was inevitable that this text should influence the way the story of this episode in the childhood of Jesus was told, particularly the emphasis on the aspect of divine care and protection. Such literary coloring has given rise in some quarters to the belief that Matthew 2 is a biblical midrash. By which is meant that the *Passover Haggadah* inspired the creation of the Flight-Return story with a view to suggesting that Jesus relived the foundational experience of his people, and thus should be seen as the New Israel. The fundamental flaw in this approach is that it confuses form and content. What is obviously true for the form is erroneously assumed to be true for the content. Matthew 2 borrows the form of the *Passover Haggadah*, but definitely not the content, because in this case Jesus would have been depicted as an adult in order to wear the haggadic mantle of Jacob. The hypothesis of pure creativity cannot explain why Jesus is depicted *as a child*. Thus a fact of his childhood stands at the beginning of the development process, and it is this that we must now question.

The Historicity of the Flight to Egypt

It is extremely doubtful that Herod the Great had the slightest interest in the child Jesus. A child could neither plot nor threaten, and Herod was now so ill that it is inconceivable that he would want to take out a potential enemy a generation into the future. His concern was with imminent danger, and in this respect Bethlehem certainly concerned him deeply.

Throughout his life Herod had to contend with enemies. To protect himself, Josephus tells us,

> there were spies set everywhere both in the city and on the roads who watched those who met together; it is even reported that he did not neglect this part of caution, but that he would sometimes disguise himself as a private individual and mix among the multitude in the night time in order to test what opinion they had of his rule. (AJ 15.366-67)

In 7 B.C.E. Herod had his sons Alexander and Aristobulus executed on suspicion of treason. In 5 B.C.E. Herod learned that another son, Antipater, had conspired to poison him. Late that year when he became ill, there was a tentative uprising in Jerusalem. Herod burned the ringleaders alive, and had the others executed (JW 1.647-55).

Under these conditions it would be extraordinary if Herod had not taken very seriously the prophecy of a warrior king who would come from Bethlehem,

> But you, O Bethlehem of Ephrathah,
> who are one of the little clans of Judah,
> from you shall come forth for me
> one who is to rule in Israel. (Micah 5:2)

From Herod's perspective this was incitement to rebellion. An opponent could recruit forces much more easily if he claimed to be the promised Messiah from Bethlehem. As God's Chosen One he was guaranteed success; he could not lose. It would be extremely naive to imagine that Herod's secret police were not all over Bethlehem just waiting for someone to step out of line.

Since Herod was prepared to execute his own sons on mere suspicion, one did not have to be a genius to realize that he would have no compunction about wiping out a whole village just to give himself peace of mind. In 37 B.C.E., at the beginning of his career, Herod had all the members of the Sanhedrin executed, because it had once dared to charge him with murder when he was governor of Galilee (AJ 14.175).

Given what everyone knew about Herod's character and temperament, it would be incredible if those who could leave Bethlehem and seek safety outside Herod's jurisdiction did not avail of the opportunity. Egypt was the traditional place of refuge for those in danger in Judea (1 Kgs 11:40; 2 Kgs 25:25-26; Jer 26:20-21), and it was not very far away. By the ancient roads it would have taken only three or four days to cover the 100 or so miles from Bethlehem to the Wadi el-Arish, "the River of Egypt" (1 Kgs 8:65; Jdt 1:9), the traditional border between Egypt and Judah. Once across that border they would have been in a Roman province, on whose territory Herod would never intrude.

Joseph's skill as an artisan gave him mobility. He could find work anywhere. He was not tied to land as were the farmers and shepherds. There can be no doubt about the historicity of the flight into Egypt of Jesus and his family. In fact, I would be extremely surprised if they were the only ones to flee from Bethlehem.

Settlement in Galilee

We have no way of knowing where the Holy Family lived in Egypt, or how long they had to stay there before Herod died. The Flight-Return source informed Matthew that the Holy Family did return to the land of Israel on getting news of the death of the king. At that point Matthew was able to supplement his source by what had become common knowledge. Joseph and his family did not return to Bethlehem, but instead took up residence in Nazareth, far to the north in Galilee.

There are two issues here. Why did Joseph avoid Bethlehem where he had a house and friends? And why did he opt for Nazareth as an alternative?

Matthew answers the first question, "when Joseph heard that Archelaus reigned over Judea in place of his father Herod, he was afraid to go there" (2:22). It is possible that Matthew had specific information regarding Joseph's motivation. But if he did not, his explanation is eminently plausible.

Even before he went to Rome to claim his inheritance, Archelaus slew three thousand of those who opposed him (JW 2.1-13). His reputation was so bad that a Jewish delegation was sent to Rome from Jerusalem to beg the emperor Augustus not to approve his nomination as king (JW 2.80-92). Augustus, however, went ahead as regards the land willed to Archelaus, but denied him the royal title (JW 2.93). While all this was going on in Rome, the Roman general P. Quinctilius Varus, the Roman governor of Syria, had to stamp out a rebellion in Palestine. At the end of his campaign he crucified two thousand (JW 2.66-79). Even the most politically unaware could see that was not the time to return to Judea, particularly since the expected consequences of Archelaus' disappointment were fully realized when he returned home. "He used not only the Jews, but also the Samaritans, barbarously, and this out of resentment at their old quarrels with him" (JW 2.111). Clearly the inhabitants of Bethlehem would have been in even greater danger than in the days of Herod the Great. Archelaus had to face greater opposition than his father, and so had good reason to fear the appearance of a Messiah from Bethlehem.

Matthew gives us no answer to the second question, but it is highly probable that Joseph's choice of Nazareth was motivated by economic considerations.

Herod's will gave Galilee to another son, Antipas. He, however, inherited a kingdom without a capital. In putting down the rebellion that followed Herod's death in 4 B.C.E., Varus burnt Sepphoris to the ground (JW 2.68). Antipas' first concern was to rebuild Sepphoris bigger and more beautiful in emulation of his father, who had built new cities at Caesarea, Antipatris, and Phasaelis, in addition to rebuilding Sebaste and Agrippias.[3] The original size of Sepphoris is unknown, but Antipas planned for a population of twenty-five thousand.[4]

Once word went out that Antipas was recruiting a labor force, Joseph realized he would have work on the site for ten to twelve years, the average period for the building of a Herodian city (AJ 15.341; 16.136). It would be unwise, however, to put his wife and children in the rough conditions of a great international work camp. Nazareth, only four kilometers away, was clearly visible to the west across the valley. There his family could live undisturbed for the price of an hour's walk to work. And there he could develop a second business to which his sons (Mark 6:3) could contribute.

Villages, however, are notoriously unreceptive to newcomers. There would have been no overt hostility, but neither would there have been the warm welcome that would make the refugees from Bethlehem feel at home. For a year, perhaps longer, they would have been regarded with suspicion. Was Joseph an agent of the new king? Might he be reporting to the tax collectors? Patiently he and his family had to win their place in a new society. Through the proximity of Nazareth to Sepphoris, the growing Jesus was subject to influences he would never have experienced in Bethlehem, but that is matter for the next chapter.

Paul

It is an extraordinary coincidence that the circumstances that brought Jesus to Galilee were precisely those that forced Paul and his family into exile.

It is a further coincidence that Luke made the same mistake regarding the origins of both Jesus and Paul. Jesus was known as Jesus of Nazareth. Hence, Luke assumed that his parents were natives of Nazareth, and that his birth in Bethlehem was an accident. Matthew tells a more accurate story (see chapter 1). Similarly, Paul was known as Paul of Tarsus, and Luke in consequence assumed that he had been born there (Acts 22:3), but there is good reason to think he acquired the name simply because he grew up there, just as Jesus got his name because he grew up in Nazareth.

If Matthew's version of the origins of Jesus contradicts that of Luke, so the latter's account of the origins of Paul is contradicted by Jerome of Bethlehem. In 387 or 388 he wrote a commentary on Paul's letter to Philemon in which he said apropos of verses 23-24:

> They say that the parents of the Apostle Paul were from Gischala, a region of Judea and that, when the whole province was devastated by the hand of Rome and the Jews scattered throughout the world, they were moved to Tarsus a town of Cilicia; the boy Paul inherited the lot of his parents. Thus we can understand what he says of himself "Are they Hebrews? So am I. Are they Israelites? So am I. Are they seed of Abraham? So am I" (2 Cor 11:22), and also elsewhere "A Hebrew born of Hebrews" (Phil 3:5), and other things which suggest that he was much more a Judean than a Tarsian. (PL 26.617)

Four or five years later Jerome wrote a biographical dictionary of 135 Christian authors entitled *Famous Men*. Naturally Paul figured prominently; his biography is the fifth and opens with the words,

Paul, an apostle, previously called Saul, was not one of the Twelve Apostles. He was of the tribe of Benjamin and of the town of Gischala in Judea. When the town was captured by the Romans, he migrated with his parents to Tarsus in Cilicia. (TU 14.9)

The unqualified affirmation that Paul was a Palestinian is found in no other source. In consequence, these two texts must be examined closely. There is only one Gischala in Palestine. Today known as el-Jish in Arabic and as Gush Halav in modern Hebrew, it is located some five kilometers north of Mount Meiron in Upper Galilee. The name means "Fat Soil" and Gischala was famous for its olive oil.[5]

In Defense of Jerome

The fact that Gischala is located in Galilee, not in Judea, cannot be used as an argument to discredit Jerome. Even in the New Testament "Judea" is used with two distinct meanings. In the narrow sense Judea is distinguished from Galilee and Samaria (Luke 2:4; Acts 9:31). In the wider sense of "land of the Jews" the term englobes Galilee, e.g., "the word which was proclaimed throughout all Judea beginning from Galilee" (Acts 10:37; cf. Luke 1:5; 23:5). For the Romans from 70 c.e. onwards, the whole area under their control was simply Judea,[6] and this is the usage Jerome and his contemporaries inherited.

The tension between the classification of Gischala as first a "region" and then a "town" is more apparent than real. Gischala was in fact a town. But it served as the principal market for the surrounding area that inevitably took its name from the urban center. Moreover, Jerome was not particularly interested in geography, and had little personal knowledge of sites in Palestine.[7] Hence, a mistake in his commentary on Philemon is understandable. In the interval between this work and *Famous Men*, however, Jerome had translated and updated the *Onomasticum* (a gazetteer of places mentioned in the Bible) of Eusebius of Caesarea that focused his attention on topography. At the same time Jerome was working on his *Hebraicae Quaestiones in Libro Geneseos*, in which he drew freely on Josephus, "the only non-Christian historian he knew thoroughly and whom he had hailed as the Greek Livy."[8] Gischala appears frequently as a city in the writings of Josephus because it was the home of his detested enemy John ben Levi. Thus, it is not surprising that Gischala should be correctly identified as a town in *Famous Men*.

Where did Jerome get the information about Paul's origins that appears in his commentary on Philemon? In all probability from Origen, whose commentary on Philemon unfortunately is no longer extant.[9] Origen must have relied on an oral tradition he considered trustworthy. I am forced to the same conclusion. Certainly it is impossible to think why anyone should invent Gischala as Paul's birthplace. It is not even mentioned in the Bible. Paul identifies himself as a Benjaminite, but Gischala is far outside the northern border of the territory of the tribe of Benjamin. Gischala had no connection with the ministry of Jesus in Galilee, and it had no Christian population in the Byzantine period. In other words, there was nothing to spark invention, and creativity conferred no benefit on anyone.

An Aramaic Speaker

It is also extremely interesting that Jerome considered 2 Corinthians 11:22 and Philippians 3:5 as confirmation of Paul's Palestinian origins. In both these texts Paul identifies himself both as an "Israelite" / "of the people of Israel" and a "Hebrew." The two terms overlap to a considerable extent, and they were used interchangeably at the time of Paul to identify a Jew. It is most unusual, however, to find them used together as here, and the assumption must be that in Paul's mind one added something to the other. "Israelite" means belonging to Israel, a member of the people of God, and nothing else. "Hebrew," on the other hand, is often used inaccurately in the New Testament to mean the language spoken by Jews in Palestine. Luke, for example, depicts Paul speaking to the Jerusalem crowd "in the Hebrew language" (Acts 21:40; 22:2; 26:14) by which he must have meant Aramaic, the spoken tongue. The vast majority of Jews knew no Hebrew. To make the Hebrew text of the Scriptures intelligible to them it had to be translated into Aramaic in the synagogue. This is confirmed by John who claimed that the words "Gabbatha" (19:13; the place where Pilate condemned Jesus), and "Golgotha" (19:17) were Hebrew, when in fact they are Aramaic.[10] Thus the division between "Hebrews" and "Hellenists" among the first Christian converts in Jerusalem was between Aramaic speakers and those whose language was Greek (Acts 6:1).

In both 2 Corinthians 11:22 and Philippians 3:5, therefore, Paul is proudly claiming to be an Aramaic-speaking Jew who had inherited the language from his parents. As Jerome astutely noted, the immediate inference is that his parents at least had lived in Palestine. Diaspora Jews had no need of Aramaic. They used whatever local dialect was necessary for daily living, and learned Greek in order to communicate with a wider world. They did not use the Aramaic targums, but a Greek translation of the Scriptures known as the Septuagint.

Was Jerome, or Origen for that matter, interested only in explaining how Paul knew Aramaic, the obvious thing to do would have been to appeal to the fact that he was educated in Jerusalem. Paul himself tells us that he had studied Pharisaism there as a young man (Gal 1:14; Phil 3:5). Luke claims that he was a schoolboy there (Acts 22:3; 26:4), which, as we shall see, is not in fact correct. That neither Jerome nor Origen made use of such texts strongly suggests they accepted Gischala as an unavoidable fact.

Budget Slavery

According to both of Jerome's texts, Paul and his parents were forced out of Gischala by the Romans, who deported them to Tarsus. When did this take place and why? In terms of what we have seen above regarding the date of Paul's birth (chapter 1), it is most probable that it was during the disturbances that followed the death of Herod in 4 B.C.E.

The rebellion in Galilee was led by Judas, son of Hezekiah, who armed his supporters by breaking into the arsenal of Sepphoris (AJ 17.271). In response the Roman general, Varus, "took the city of Sepphoris and burnt it, and made slaves of the inhabitants" (JW 2.68). The last point does not mean that the citizens became prisoners of war to be liberated once peace had been established. The Romans sold them as slaves and used the money as a contribution to their campaign expenses.

This was standard practice. When Cassius Longinus, in his first administration of Syria (53–51 B.C.E.) was short of money, "he made a swift march into Judea, and after taking Tariceae, he carried away 30,000 Jews into slavery" (JW 1.180). Incidentally, this text is significant confirmation of Jerome's usage, because Tariceae (otherwise called Magdala), a city on the Sea of Galilee, is said to be in Judea. During Cassius Longinus' second administration (44–42 B.C.E.), when the Jewish inhabitants of Gophna, Emmaus, Lydda, and Thamna failed to pay their taxes, he took the money out of their hides by selling them as slaves (AJ 14.275). Writing around the middle of the first century C.E., Philo says that the Trastevere district of Rome was occupied by Jews who for the most part were "Roman citizens, having been emancipated; for, having been brought as captives into Italy, they were manumitted by those who bought them for slaves" (*Legatio ad Gaium* 155). Hadrian paid for the long and arduous suppression of the Bar Kokhba revolt by selling so many slaves that the market was glutted.[11]

We must assume, therefore, that the inhabitants of Sepphoris were not the only ones sold into slavery by order of Varus, and that Paul's parents were somehow taken by one of the Roman patrols sent out to collect as many able-bodied individuals as the finance officer of the legion deemed necessary to balance his budget. This is not confirmed by what Josephus tells us about the fate of Gischala (JW 4.84-120), but he makes it clear that the situation was so confused that Paul's parents could have been picked up virtually anywhere. A female slave was valued as highly as a male because her children were slaves.

Before returning to their base at Antioch-on-the-Orontes (modern Antakya in southern Turkey) the legions would have sold their captives to the omnipresent slave traders who closely followed every campaign (1 Macc 3:41; 2 Macc 8:11). Philo condemns those "who, for the sake of lawless gain sell slaves to slave dealers, and enslave them to any chance persons, transporting them to a foreign land, so that they shall never any more salute their native land, not even in a dream, or taste of any hope of happiness" (*De spec. leg.* 4.17; trans. Yonge). For the dealers, however, slaves were just another type of cargo. In the Apocalypse, merchants lament that "no one buys their cargo any more, cargo of gold, silver, jewels and pearls, fine linen . . . cattle and sheep, horses and chariots, and bodies and human souls" (18:11-13). "Body" (*sôma*) was a common synonym for "slave" (*doulos*),[12] and here appears at the bottom of a descending scale of value. Slaves were just a commodity like other animals to be sold where the demand was greatest.

The baby Paul and his parents were probably shipped out of the nearest port, Ptolemais (modern Akko in northern Israel). As the slave ships worked their way north along the coast, it would not have been good business to have all the ships arrive together at any given port. Prices fell quickly in a saturated market. The slave dealers must have arranged among themselves to divide or stagger their landfalls.

How many times did Paul's parents experience the degradation of being driven to market, the shame of being offered for sale, before the final humiliation of being handed over to a master? No matter how young Paul was, he sensed the emotions of his parents, and was marked by the experience for life. As he grew up and learned from his Aramaic-speaking parents how they came to be residents of Tarsus, he relived their pain.

Given what Paul went through as the young child of slaves, it is striking that he should have built his vision of reality on two extraordinary paradoxes. What the vast majority of the free thought of as liberty he insisted is in fact slavery (Gal 4:9; Rom 6:17). Genuine freedom is achieved through a transaction common in the slave markets. "You do not belong to yourselves for you were bought with a price" (1 Cor 6:19-20).

Notes

[1] David Daube, "The Earliest Structure of the Gospels," *New Testament Studies* 5 (1958) 174–75.

[2] L. Finkelstein, "The Oldest Midrash: Pre-Rabbinic Ideals and Teaching in the Passover Haggadah," *Harvard Theological Review* 31 (1938) 291–317.

[3] Peter Richardson, *Herod. King of the Jews and Friend of the Romans* (Columbia, SC: University of South Carolina Press, 1996) 177.

[4] Harold Hoehner, *Herod Antipas* (Grand Rapids, MI: Zondervan, 1972) 52.

[5] Emil Schürer, *The History of the Jewish People in the Age of Jesus Christ (175 BC–AD 135)* (Edinburgh: Clark, 1973–87) 496.

[6] Ibid., 514.

[7] John Wilkinson, "L'apport de saint Jérôme à la topographie," *Revue Biblique* 81 (1974) 245–57.

[8] J.N.D. Kelly, *Jerome. His Life, Writings, and Controversies* (London: Duckworth, 1975) 153–56.

[9] Ibid., 145–49.

[10] Schürer, *The History of the Jewish People in the Age of Jesus Christ,* 2:22.

[11] Ibid., 1:553.

[12] Jennifer Glancy, *Slavery in Early Christianity* (Oxford: Oxford University Press, 2002) 10.

Chapter 3

Adapting to an Alien Environment: Sepphoris and Tarsus

*B*oth Jesus and Paul were refugees in their childhood. This traumatic experience certainly influenced them for the rest of their lives. In both instances, however, deportation meant that they grew up in places that gave them advantages they would never have enjoyed had they stayed in remote country villages such as Bethlehem and Gischala.

Everything Nazareth had to offer could have been found in Bethlehem with one major exception. Nazareth was within sight and easy reach of Sepphoris, the new capital of Galilee, ruled by a cosmopolitan and Romanophile king. It was in microcosm the complex world of the eastern Mediterranean. The mountain village of Gischala had absolutely nothing in common with the great city of Tarsus, which lay on a major east-west trade route and was home to one of the great rhetorical schools in the Greco-Roman world.

The doors that Nazareth and Tarsus opened to Jesus and Paul respectively certainly enlarged their minds, but they also permitted alien elements into their lives that complicated the process of growing up. They both had to confront choices that did not present themselves to Jews in more sheltered environments.

Jesus

Herod Antipas, as we have seen, had to rebuild Sepphoris after its destruction by Varus in 4 B.C.E. What sort of a city would he have built? In answering, the culture and personality of Antipas must be decisive.

When Antipas became tetrarch of Galilee, he was only sixteen years old.[1] Like his older brothers, his father Herod the Great had sent him to Rome (AJ 17.20) as soon as he became an adult Jew at the age of twelve or thirteen to be educated in the house of a certain Pollio (AJ 15.342). His father's intention was that he should stay in Rome for five or so years and in the process learn everything possible about the Romans, and in particular the imperial family, with whom he would have to deal for the rest of his life.

Roman Education

Antipas' studies were cut short after some three years by a summons from his father to return to Judea. This was probably a consequence of Herod's decision in 5 B.C.E. to name him his sole successor (JW 1.646). It would have been natural to want to talk to him about the future and his conduct of policy.[2] However, only four or five days before his death, Herod again changed his will, probably realizing the emperor would not accept a sixteen year old as ruler of a vast realm that was also of great strategic importance.[3] Under this new will, Antipas received only Galilee and Peraea (JW 1.664). Despite his immaturity at the beginning, Antipas proved worthy of the trust and ruled relatively well for forty-three years. Jesus called him "that fox" (Luke 13:32), an epithet that conveys grudging respect for a cunning survivor. He was of milder temperament than his father and devoid of paranoia. His only mistake was his marriage to Herodias, his half-brother Philip's wife (Mark 6:15), who fostered the ambition that would be his downfall.

Antipas' tutor in Rome was a remarkable personality who cannot have failed to influence an impressionable young man. Gaius Asinius Pollio (76 B.C.E.–4 C.E.) was an almost exact contemporary of Herod the Great. After a successful military career he served as consul in 40 B.C.E. The following year he defeated the Parthini in Illyria, and after his triumph retired from politics to devote himself principally to the study of history (OCD 192). He also wrote poetry and tragedy, and counted Catullus, Horace, and Virgil among his friends. His greatest contribution, however, flowed from his practical bent and concern for the common good. Following up on a project of Julius Caesar (Suetonius, *Caesar*, 44), which had been aborted by the latter's assassination in 43 B.C.E., he used his personal wealth to build the first public library in Rome sometime in the 30s B.C.E. It had two sections, one for works in Greek, the other for works in Latin.[4] Its nucleus no doubt came from his own personal collection, but the layout of the library demanded careful planning. He had to find a way to conserve and yet make easily accessible hundreds of rolls of parchment and papyrus, while at the same time providing facilities for readers. His solution was so brilliant that it influenced the emperor Augustus when he built the Palatine Library attached to the Temple of Apollo in 28 B.C.E.[5]

Pollio was someone that Antipas could both respect and admire. He was a man of action, and at the same time a creative intellectual. His integrity was such that he did not fear to criticize the emperor when he thought it necessary. In other words, he was an ideal role model, presumably why Herod chose him to instruct his sons. Certainly Antipas saw in Pollio the best qualities of an authentic Roman, and perhaps for the first time understood why throughout his life his father Herod had been so utterly consistent in his commitment to Rome. The personality of Pollio would have given reality to what had previously been only a vague perception.

Building a New City

Therefore, when Antipas came to construct a city his father would have admired, there can be little doubt that, in addition to his father's creations, e.g., Caesarea Maritima, he had in his mind's eye the Rome that Pollio had brought to life for him. Moreover, Antipas had access to the same sort of cosmopolitan building and engineering talent that had brought into being the cities of his father. These would have been Roman trained either directly or indirectly. It had been drilled into them that infrastructure was as important as appearances. Thus their first concern in a new city was for the water supply. There had to be reservoirs from which clean water was led in a network of pipes to baths, toilets, and drinking fountains. Then the number of streets, and the size of the blocks created by the streets crossing at right angles had to be decided. The width of the streets with a sidewalk on either side determined the size of the sewer below.

Elements as simple and as fundamental as these would have been wonders to Joseph and his older sons (Mark 6:3). The villages to which they were accustomed were completely unplanned and had no such facilities. Even the mansions of Sepphoris with their central courtyards would have been very different from the little houses they knew. Thus, from the time Jesus could assimilate family conversations, he would have been forced to realize that Sepphoris was a very different world compared to his village. In Nazareth, Jesus received the minimal education of all Jewish boys. In particular he learned to read and mastered the Scriptures (John 7:15). That, however, he could have done in Bethlehem. My concern here is to evoke what he gained from his proximity to Sepphoris.

As Sepphoris grew, so did the web of symbiotic relations that bound it to Nazareth. As the nearest village sited on the edge of an immensely fertile valley, Nazareth had a built-in economic advantage. Its proximity to a city reduced transport costs and made it profitable to grow the high-value, labor-intensive perishable garden crops that were indispensable to the markets of Sepphoris. The city in return provided the villagers with employment as well as with goods and services not available at home. It was there they paid taxes and used courts and the banks (Matt 25:27)—and heard the news of a wider world.

A Boy in Sepphoris

Jesus' awareness of the importance of Sepphoris in the lives of his parents no doubt fueled his curiosity. It was not a remote mystery. He could see it across the valley. To a village boy the city held the attraction of a theme park, a cornucopia of sights and sounds that excited wonder and inspired questions. Why did an arch stay up when carpenters removed the scaffolding? How could a couple of men with a crane raise a large block of stone? How did masons ensure that a wall was absolutely vertical? How did engineers transfer a line of sight to paper? Sepphoris seethed with a vitality he could almost reach out and touch. Home was unbearably dull by comparison.

It would be a great mistake to imagine that Jesus did not spend what time he could in Sepphoris from the moment he was free to explore with his friends. Long before there was a question of him assisting Joseph at work, little boys would have been making a nuisance of themselves by getting in the way of hard-working men. The invective with which they were blasted by the polyglot workforce was their introduction to Greek. The more time Jesus spent in Sepphoris, the more likely it is he would have picked up a smattering of Greek. It was the common language that enabled workers from many different backgrounds to communicate.

Another attraction for adults as well as children would have been the public shows Antipas organized. We have no concrete details, but such claims to glory were in the blood that he inherited from Herod the Great, who built the first theaters in Palestine (Jerusalem, Sebaste, Jericho, Caesarea) in addition to hippodromes, stadia, and amphitheaters. In the few years Antipas spent in Rome, he must have been impressed by the displays Augustus organized with great frequency (Suetonius, *Augustus*, 43).

Sepphoris would be inconceivable without a theater. If the still-visible forty-five-hundred-seat stone theater is not to be dated to the time of Antipas, it was certainly preceded by a wooden theater. Jews were actively discouraged from attending the theater, where all the productions were pagan in origin and content. Jesus no doubt would have heard the criticisms and warnings, which were in themselves informative, but in the vicinity of the theater he could well have seen actors in their robes pacing up and down, practicing their lines.

This is the context in which Jesus would have learned the word *hypokritês*, which is certainly not rural language. Its original meaning is entirely positive, "a public speaker," and in Attic Greek, "an actor." Jesus, however, used it in the transferred sense of "dissembler" (Mark 7:6; Matt 7:5 = Luke 6:42). This meaning does appear in two passages of the Greek translation of the Old Testament (Job 34:30; 36:13) and in Sirach 1:29, but this is not the text of the Scriptures that would have been read in the Aramaic-speaking synagogue of Nazareth. Later, when forced with the need to criticize religious leaders who honored God with their lips but not with their hearts, Jesus reached back into his memory of actors at Sepphoris, mouthing words that did not represent their thoughts, and wearing robes to which they had no right.

The greatest party of all during Jesus' association with Sepphoris would undoubtedly have been the marriage of Antipas to a daughter of the Nabataean king, Aretas IV of Petra (ruled 9 B.C.E.–40 C.E.). It is not known where or when this marriage was celebrated. It is most improbable, however, that it was long delayed after Antipas reached marriageable age, which ideally was between eighteen and twenty (*m. Aboth* 5:21). In the case of Antipas, this would have been about 2 C.E., certainly not much later. In all probability the choice was dictated by the emperor Augustus, who saw dynastic marriages as the cement of political stability (Suetonius, *Augustus* 48). Peraea, which belonged to Antipas, touched the northern boundary of Nabataea, which Aretas controlled, and there had long been bad blood between Jews and Nabataeans.[6] Augustus certainly did not want the hostility that had obtained between the fathers to be continued by the sons.

Even if the wedding was celebrated in Petra, a great caravan of Nabataean nobles would have formed part of the procession that escorted Antipas when he brought his bride back to Sepphoris. All the surrounding villages would have gathered to salute their ruler. At this time Jesus would have been at least six years old, just the age to be intrigued as he saw for the first time the burnoose-shrouded riders sitting high on the slow-striding camels. He would not then have known that the casual arrogance with which they flexed to the rhythm of the camel's gait was rooted in their control of the immensely profitable Incense and Spice Road from Yemen across Arabia to the port of Gaza (Pliny, *Natural History* 12.64-65). To him they were simply mysterious strangers whose presence stimulated questions regarding a new world out to the east that balanced the western world that he had begun to know.

Such occasions among others would have brought home to Jesus that not everyone was Jewish, and that there were alternatives to a Jewish lifestyle. It was a moment of awareness, however, not of choice. The Sepphoris that Jesus knew was a rather observant Jewish city. Despite extensive excavations, to date there is no evidence of such pagan institutions as temples, shrines, or gymnasia. Statues are nonexistent, as are pig bones in the middens. Ritual baths and stone vessels, on the contrary, are common. The small resident pagan population would have been augmented when the theater produced plays, and by the regular visits of merchants or tourists eager to see "the ornament of all Galilee" (AJ 18.27).

The Virgin Birth

The choices Sepphoris offered the growing Jesus were complicated by another factor, his mother Mary. According to Matthew, Mary was a virgin when Jesus was born. Joseph is told by the angel, "Do not fear to take Mary your wife, for that which is conceived in her is of the Holy Spirit" (1:20). Certain scholars dismiss the historicity of the virgin birth on the grounds that the Greco-Roman world was full of myths of gods copulating with women to beget heroes.[7] Others, rather more scientifically, have looked closely at the details of the stories, and correctly concluded that "there is no exact parallel or antecedent in the material available to the Christians of the first century who told of this conception [of Jesus]."[8] The principal points of difference are: (a) there is no hint in Matthew of sexual intercourse, and (b) none of the Greco-Roman stories mention the virginity of the mother, which is stressed by Matthew.

Another important point is not always taken into account. The god–woman stories that were in circulation[9] are not only polytheistic, but to a great extent pornographic, with a snake representing the penis. Even if they knew such stories, which cannot be assumed, it is inconceivable that Jewish-Christians would consider them an appropriate vehicle to say something about Jesus.

Those who claim the virgin birth is a *theologumenon* have the obligation to say what it was intended to convey about Jesus. Although formulations differ, such authors agree that Matthew's point was to highlight Jesus' divine sonship.[10] This can hardly be correct. One has only to read *The Book of Jubilees* to realize the extent to which every first-century Jew thought of Adam and Eve as historical individuals. They have sex (3:6) and are subject to the purity laws (3:9-11). Yet, even though Adam was created directly by God, no one ever thought of him as one with God in divinity. Eve might have been thought to have had one parent, because God used Adam's rib (Gen 2:21-22), but once again there is no hint that anyone considered her to be a divine child. In consequence, the virgin birth story would not have led any contemporary Jew to conclude that Jesus was divine.

The suggestion that the virgin birth story was invented to exalt the value of virginity is completely anachronistic. Virginity was of great concern to Christians from the second century c.e. onwards, but it was of nothing but the most practical interest to first-century Jews. It was imperative that a girl should be a virgin when she was married (*m. Ketuboth* 1:7), but thereafter she was expected to have sex and produce children. In fact, virginity is not even the point of the virgin birth story.

Finally, the author of the postulated *theologumenon* lived in a cynical world that automatically looked for the worst interpretation. The invention of a virgin birth story ran the danger of it being interpreted as a cover-up for Mary's adultery—precisely what happened to the virgin birth story in Jewish circles. Why would any early Christian theologian take such a risk, particularly when a virgin birth story actually said nothing about Jesus?

The historicity of the virgin birth cannot be established positively, but the extreme improbability that it is a theological creation makes its factuality a more appropriate starting point for the historian. What this means is that, if the virgin birth is a fact, Mary must have given her consent. It could not have happened without her knowledge. This is the point that Luke is making in his account of the annunciation to Mary by the angel Gabriel (1:26-35). Luke, however, has the angel supply her with information about the future of Jesus that she cannot have had at the time of conception, or for some considerable time thereafter. Mary's criticism of Jesus, "He is out of his mind" (Mark 3:21), clearly shows that she did not understand his vocation.[11] The absolute minimum required by Mary's consent is that she understood that God had chosen Jesus for a special destiny, but knew nothing of the details.

The Quest for Knowledge

We must assume, in consequence, that as soon as Jesus was capable of assimilating her message, Mary told him that God had chosen him specially. To the dismay of Jesus, however, she could give no further specification. She simply did not know why he had been selected or what he was expected to achieve. No doubt she encouraged Jesus to pray for enlightenment, and to be attentive to any and every sign that might be an indication of God's will. Thereafter, Jesus lived in a heightened state of alertness, which, as time went on, became a burden. He could never relax fully, nor could he make any decision about his future, until he knew what God wanted of him.

It was in this fraught state of mind that Jesus undertook his first journey to Jerusalem.

> (41) Now his parents went to Jerusalem every year at the feast of Passover. (42) And when he was twelve years old, they went up according to the custom of the feast. (43) And when the feast was ended, and they were returning, the boy Jesus stayed behind in Jerusalem. And his parents did not know it, (44) but supposing him to be in the caravan, they went a day's journey, and sought him among their relatives and acquaintances. (45) And when they did not find him, they returned to Jerusalem seeking him. (46) And it came to pass that after three days they found him in the temple, sitting among the teachers, both listening to them and asking them questions. (47) But all who heard him were amazed at his intelligence and his answers. (48) And seeing him they were astonished. And his mother said to him, "Child, why have you treated us so? Behold, your father and I have been seeking you anxiously." (49) And he said to them, "Why did you seek me? Did you know that I must be about my Father's business?" (50) And they did not understand what he said to them. (51) And he went down with them and came to Nazareth. (Luke 2:41-51)

The use of "his parents" does not necessarily betray ignorance of the virgin birth. Certainly Luke did not think so. It is a natural simplification that appears earlier in 2:27 ("his parents") and 2:33 ("his father and mother"). It would be very awkward to repeat the cumbersome "his mother and his supposed father" (cf. Luke 3:23).

What is really remarkable is that we are told that Mary and Joseph made the Passover pilgrimage to Jerusalem (Exod 23:14-17) "every year" and stayed for the full eight days of the feast (Lev 23:5-6). This means that Joseph was wealthy enough to sacrifice three weeks' earnings. Well-organized merchants used to traveling quickly could make the trip from Galilee to Jerusalem in perhaps four days. A straggling caravan of men, women, and children motivated only by piety would take at least a week in each direction. Moreover, Joseph could afford to bring his wife with him, even though she was not obliged to go. If Luke is correct, Joseph's social class and economic level were somewhat higher than the modern blue-collar worker in lower middle-class America, which is the estimate of John Meier.[12]

A Jewish boy was considered a responsible adult on completion of his thirteenth year (*m. Aboth* 5:21; *m. Niddah* 5:6), and so was obliged to observe the Law. There is some reason to think that pious Jews obliged their sons to obey the commandments one or two years before it was strictly necessary so that obedience might have become habitual by the time it was required (*m. Yoma* 8:4).

Thus it is entirely possible that Mary and Joseph took the initiative of bringing Jesus to Jerusalem when he was twelve years old. I strongly suspect, however, that Jesus argued to be permitted to go with them. He still did not know what God had in mind for him, and the following year he would be an adult, and perhaps culpable in the case of failure. Certainly it is only in this perspective that we can understand why he overstayed in Jerusalem to hear and question the teachers in the Temple (v. 46).

It would not be reasonable to assume that a twelve-year-old boy had an overriding interest in theology for its own sake. That simply cannot be taken for granted. If it was just idle curiosity regarding a possible future career, Jesus had had seven days in which to test the water. The determination of Jesus to prolong the contact with the teachers, even at the risk of disobedience to his parents, reveals that he was not getting the answer he desperately needed. If his mother could not tell him what his destiny was, the only possible alternative was the experts in the Law who articulated the will of God for all Jews. And he would not leave them until he was absolutely sure they had nothing to give him.

The following verse, "But all who heard him were astonished at his intelligence and his answers" (v. 47), cannot be construed as an objection to this hypothesis, because it did not belong to the original story. There are three strong arguments. (a) In contrast to "and" *(kai)* with which all the other sentences except verse 44 begin, verse 47 is introduced by "but" *(de)*. (b) Jesus answers questions that have not been asked, and that have not been implied by verse 46. (c) Most importantly, the grammatical antecedent of "seeing him they were astonished" (v. 48) is "all who heard him" (v. 47). There is no indication of any change of subject. Yet, from what follows in verse 48 it is clear that "seeing him they were astonished" is a reference to Mary and Joseph, who are also the subjects of "they found him" in verse 46. Therefore, verse 47 is a secondary interpolation[13] that not only burdens the narrative with a completely alien theme, but distracts from the statement of Jesus in verse 49, which is the point of the narrative.

The purpose of the insertion in verse 47 is to give Jesus an active role. The precocious intelligence of a child is a standard element in the novelistic technique of the enhancement of the hero. Similar stories are told of Moses (AJ 2.230), of Alexander the Great (Plutarch, *Alexander* 5), and of Apollonius of Tyana (Philostratus, *Life*, 7). Josephus even has the cheek to say of himself, "When I was a child, about 14 years of age . . . the chief priests and principal men of the city frequently came to me together in order to know the accurate interpretation of points of the law" (*Life*, 9).

Having finished with the distraction caused by verse 47, we return to the narrative. Mary's reproachful question (v. 48) evokes surprise on the part of Jesus (v. 49). His parents should have known better. Why? Because they were aware of the question preoccupying Jesus.

The Greek of Jesus' second question reads *ouk êdeite hoti en tois tou patros mou dei einai me*. It can be translated in two ways: "Did you not know that I must be in my Father's house?" and "Did you not know that I must be involved in the affairs of my Father?" On purely linguistic grounds the first is uniformly preferred by the current translations (NRSV, NJB, NAB). The commentators who concur, however, limit their interpretations to developments of a banal contrast between Joseph's house (Jesus' apparent home) and God's house (his true home).[14]

We can go a step further by asking: what did Jesus expect to gain by staying in the Temple? Only one answer is possible: enlightenment. If his family and human teachers had failed him, then it seemed to Jesus' twelve-year-old intelligence[15] that he had a better chance of learning God's will for him by staying as close to the divine presence as possible. He undoubtedly knew that it was in a vision in the Temple that Isaiah received his vocation (6:8).

This project was so childish that his parents did not understand it (v. 50), and insisted that he return with them to Nazareth. Jesus obeyed (v.

51), no doubt with a sense of frustration, because the future seemed to be a blank in terms of avenues to understanding what God required of him. The problem was further complicated by his growing awareness of the world symbolized by Sepphoris. That frustration was to intensify because it was to be the best part of twenty years before news that a prophet was active in the lower Jordan valley filtered through to Nazareth. It provoked a surge of hope in Jesus' breast that now at last he might learn the destiny God had chosen for him. He set off to encounter John the Baptist.

Paul

Doubtless Paul's mother also told him as a child that he was special, both to God and his parents, but this was in no way parallel to the extraordinary information that Mary had given to Jesus regarding his relation to God. To this extent, therefore, their childhoods were very different. Paul did not live under the pressure to "know" that dominated the adolescence of Jesus. Nonetheless, what Jesus experienced in and through Sepphoris has very definite analogies with what Paul lived through growing up in Tarsus.

Tarsus lies some sixteen kilometers up the river Cydnus on the western edge of a huge fertile plain producing grapes and cereals, and above all flax that provided the raw material for the linen for which the area was famous. In addition it had the enormous advantage of being sited on one of the great trade routes of antiquity. Traffic from the Aegean and Anatolia came through the Cilician Gates, a narrow pass in the Taurus Mountains to the north of Tarsus, and left the plain of Cilicia via the Syrian Gates in the Amanus Mountains to the east, which carried the road on to Antioch-on-the-Orontes, the capital of Syria.

Understandably, therefore, Tarsus had a much longer and more colorful history than Sepphoris. An appropriate moment to take up its story is the autumn day in 41 B.C.E. when Cleopatra and Mark Antony met for the first time. Shakespeare offers a much more poetic rendering in *Antony and Cleopatra* (Act 2, Scene 2) of the bald facts reported by Plutarch:

> She sailed up the river Cydnus in a barge with gilded poop, its sails spread purple, its rowers urging it on with silver oars to the sound of the flute blended with pipes and lutes. She herself reclined beneath a canopy spangled with gold, adorned like Venus in a painting, while boys like Loves in paintings stood on either side and fanned

her. . . . And a rumour spread on every hand that Venus was come to revel with Bacchus for the good of Asia (*Antony* 26; trans. Perrin).[16]

This meeting of Rome and Egypt in Tarsus was just an accident of history. It is nonetheless a symbol of the city insofar as it straddled the east-west divide. The depth of its eastern roots is best demonstrated by its convention regarding feminine attire that endured into the second century C.E.: "it prescribes that women should be so arrayed and should so deport themselves when in the street that nobody could see any part of them, and that they themselves might not see anything off the road" (Dio Chrysostom, *Discourses* 33.48; trans. Crosby). The wearing of the chador at such a late date betrays a tribal conservatism that must also have manifested itself in other ways. It is strikingly at variance with the entirely western democratic constitution of the city. From the second century B.C.E. it had the status of a Greek city-state issuing its own coins and governed by elected magistrates.

With a view to promoting trade and commerce, the Seleucid overlords compensated for eastern languor by an infusion of energetic business-minded Greek and Jewish colonists. Rome also made decisive contributions to the well-being of Tarsus.

Pompey in 67 B.C.E. made it the capital of the newly established province of Cilicia, provoking the resentment of other claimants to the honor. Presumably because of his delight in Cleopatra, Mark Antony facilitated the economic growth of the city by granting it immunity from Roman taxes (Appian, *History* 5.1.7). This was an extremely rare privilege for a city that was not a Roman colony, but it was renewed after Antony's defeat in 31 B.C.E. by the victor Augustus (Dio Chrysostom, *Discourses* 34.8, 14, 25). Such significant marks of Roman interest were likely to have been accompanied by grants of Roman citizenship during the civil wars when loyalty commanded a good price. The number of Roman citizens who were also citizens of Tarsus would have increased exponentially with each succeeding generation.

Slaves in Tarsus

The city's prosperity and the fact that they could bring their ships into the middle of the city made Tarsus a most attractive market for the slave traders, who had to dispose of Paul's parents and others as quickly as possible. Otherwise they could see their profits disappearing down the throats of their commodity that had to be maintained in saleable form. Moreover, just at this point, the beginning of the first century C.E., the market for slaves began to contract because the children of women in slavery became sufficient to meet the demand for new slaves.[17]

In the American South in the seventeenth through nineteenth centuries there was complete identity between the theory and practice of slavery. Slaves were "speaking tools" and could never rise above that status. In the Greco-Roman world, on the contrary, slaves were theoretically chattels, but in practice they could become anything. An ex-slave, who had done very well for himself, had inscribed on his tombstone *Servitus mihi nunquam invida fuisti*, "Slavery was never unkind to me."[18] There was no lament for years lost, because slavery obviously had been a springboard to success.

There was such a wide variety in the ways slaves were treated that our only clue to the sort of life that Paul and his parents lived is the quality of the education he received. It will become clear that they must have been treated with the utmost leniency, and were finally freed with the priceless gift of Roman citizenship,[19] probably when Paul's father would have been in his thirties.[20] There were different ways in which the family unity could have been preserved.[21]

First, and in economic terms the most important point, Paul did not have to work. Labor conflicts with study (Ben Sira 38:24-27). Paul went to school until the end of his teens, and exhibits the typical contempt of the leisured class for manual labor (1 Cor 9:19; 2 Cor 11:7). As a teenager there can be little doubt but that he would have applauded Cicero, who wrote to his son, Marcus, then a student in Athens:

> Unbecoming to a gentleman, too, and vulgar are the means of livelihood of all hired workmen who we pay for mere manual labour, not for artistic skill; for in their case the very wages they receive is a pledge of their slavery. . . . And all artisans are engaged in vulgar trades; for no workshop can have anything liberal about it. (*De Officiis* 150–1; trans. Miller)[22]

Secondly, someone had to pay for Paul's schooling. This could have been a master who believed that education increased the value of a slave. Or it could have been Paul's parents. Under Roman law they could own nothing, but the legal convention of the *peculium* got around this, and in practice a slave could freely dispose of funds acquired in various ways, even to the point of acquiring other slaves, or buying his or her own freedom (OCD 1130).

Education

Further education would have been impossible had Paul not learned to read and write as a child. Pagan and Jewish elementary schools were available where such basic skills were inculcated from the age of five or six.[23] The Jewish population of Tarsus was certainly big enough to support at least one Jewish school, and Paul's depth of knowledge of his faith suggests that it was such that he attended. Thus from day one Paul had to learn the observances that were the basis of his religious identity, and for which he was responsible once he had completed his thirteenth year. The intensity of such indoctrination is attested for Palestine by Josephus (*Against Appion* 2.178) and for the Diaspora by Philo (*Legatio ad Gaium* 210) in almost identical words that present the commandments as graven on the soul by repetition.

Jewish schools, however, also had to educate their pupils to live in a Hellenistic world. Paul's parents may possibly have learned some Greek in Gischala, but it would have been the sort of smattering that Jesus picked up in Sepphoris. In Tarsus it was imperative to be fluent. Thus it is likely that, as in so many refugee families throughout the centuries, Paul's parents continued to speak the language of the old country, and thus passed it on to their son, but they learned the language of their new home from and with Paul. He was the one to receive systematic linguistic instruction at school, and he had the absorbent mind that makes it so easy for young children to soak up languages. Jewish children would have used the Greek translation of the Scriptures called the Septuagint as a reader. But if Homer was read in Pharisaic circles in Jerusalem,[24] then Greek literature undoubtedly formed part of the curriculum of Jewish schools in the Diaspora.[25]

The problems such exposure to the Greco-Roman world generated for a Jewish boy were compounded by the infinite variety of life in a busy commercial city that Paul encountered on his way to and from school. The greatly diversified urban population was supplemented occasionally by even more exotic figures. Those, for example, who came to market from the wild hinterland, and especially the merchants with their laden caravans passing through from east and west. The wonder and the questions stimulated by contact with a world so different from the Jewish home the boy Jesus experienced at Sepphoris were shared by Paul in Tarsus.

Paul's education certainly did not stop when he finished elementary school at the age of eleven or twelve. Secondary studies continued for at least three years more, and Paul must have stayed in school. Otherwise he would not have been prepared to go on to the third stage, the study of rhetoric, which began at the age of fourteen or fifteen. The secondary school, in addition to widening the scope of the student's reading in the Greek classics, concentrated on literary composition. The pupils were taught to write. Their papers were expected to integrate into a narrative agent, action, time, place, mode, and cause, while being brief, clear, probable, and grammatically correct.[26]

Without such rigorous formation Paul could not have progressed to third-level studies, where he attended the lectures of an orator and learned with him the art of eloquence.[27] For this, of course, a considerable fee had to be paid. Paul's extraordinary rhetorical ability is now universally recognized. His mastery of the figures of style, and the rhetorical structure of his letters can only have been the fruit of long, concentrated study and consistent practice. He was so well trained that his skills had become innate. Their application was instinctive rather than conscious. His grasp of the principles of the art of persuasion was so sure that he could parody them. In the Fool's Speech (2 Cor 11:1–12:13), for example, he inverts the structure of a speech in self-defense and totally transforms the expected content.

In the study of rhetoric it was impossible not to be exposed to philosophical speculation. That Paul did have some philosophical training is clear from his manipulation of sophisticated ideas regarding the nature of change in his treatment of the resurrection in 1 Corinthians 15.[28] He also occasionally betrays knowledge of the tenets and argumentative techniques of Stoicism.[29]

The force of these observations is to make it most probable that Paul attended what today would be called the university of Tarsus. According to Strabo,

> The people of Tarsus have devoted themselves so eagerly, not only to philosophy, but also to the whole round of education in general, that they have surpassed Athens, Alexandria, or any other place that can be named where there have been schools and lectures of philosophers. . . . Further, the city of Tarsus has all kinds of schools of rhetoric. . . . [which meant that] Tarsians have a facility whereby anyone could instantly speak off the cuff and unceasingly on any given subject. (*Geography* 14.5.13-14; trans. Jones, modified)[30]

The reputation of the school in the latter part of the first century B.C.E. was in great part due to Athenodorus. A native of Tarsus, he made a great reputation in Rome as a Stoic philosopher, and taught the emperor Augustus, who sent him to govern Tarsus after the fall of Mark Antony (OCD 203). Inevitably the university became a bastion of Stoicism. Even if Paul did not formally study it, he could not have escaped its all-pervasive influence.

One of the key ideas of Stoicism was that a spark of divine reason inhabited every human being. In consequence, social, religious, and racial distinctions were meaningless. In the last analysis the master was no different from the slave, nor the Greek from the barbarian. I have chosen this aspect in order to illustrate the sort of problem Paul had to face time and time again while a student at Tarsus. Any idealistic young man would have been attracted by the concept of universal brotherhood that the Stoics proclaimed. Paul, however, was a Jew, who believed his people had been set apart from all others. The Law of Moses under which he lived reinforced this fundamental belief by the dietary regulations designed to make close association between Jews and Gentiles difficult, if not impossible.

Like any Jew who attempted to live in both the Jewish and Gentile worlds, Paul experienced continuous tension between conflicting demands. It would be most surprising if, as a teenager, his attitude toward the Law was not ambivalent. On one hand, it severely restricted his social life. He could not even share a drink with fellow students unless he brought the bottle, because Gentile wine was forbidden to Jews. On the other hand, that Law was a source of pride that grounded his identity.

Paul would have been nineteen or twenty when he finished his course of rhetoric. Then he had to face the question that agitated Jesus at the same age. What was he to do with the rest of his life? The options open to him were conditioned by his place in the Greco-Roman world. Hitherto he had been *in* it but not *of* it, and the pressure had been unrelenting. Was that the sort of life he really wanted to live? Would not things be easier in a world to which he belonged, a society controlled by Jewish laws and customs? To test this hypothesis he set off for Jerusalem.

Notes

[1] Harold Hoehner, *Herod Antipas* (Grand Rapids, MI: Zondervan, 1972) 17.

[2] Ibid.

[3] Ibid., 276.

[4] Lionel Casson, *Libraries in the Ancient World* (New Haven, CT: Yale University Press, 2002) 80.

[5] Ibid., 81.

[6] Hoehner, *Herod Antipas,* 129–30.

[7] For example, Ulrich Luz, *Das Evangelium nach Matthäus,* 1985, 110.

[8] Raymond E. Brown, "The Problem of the Virginal Conception of Jesus," *Theological Studies 33* (1972) 30; W. D. Davies and Dale Allison, *A Critical and Exegetical Commentary on the Gospel of Matthew.* I. *Chs. 1–7,* International Critical Commentary (Edinburgh: Clark, 1988) 216.

[9] Thomas Boslooper, *The Virgin Birth* (London: SCM Press, 1962) 135–86.

[10] Davies and Allison, *A Critical and Exegetical Commentary on the Gospel of Matthew,* 220; James D. G. Dunn, *Christology in the Making. An Inquiry into the Origins of the Doctrine of the Incarnation* (London: SCM Press, 1980) 49–50.

[11] Raymond E. Brown and others, *Mary in the New Testament. A Collaborative Assessment by Protestant and Roman Catholic Scholars* (Philadelphia: Fortress/New York: Paulist, 1978) 51–59.

[12] John P. Meier, *A Marginal Jew. Rethinking the Historical Jesus.* I. *The Roots of the Problem and the Person* (New York: Doubleday, 1991) 282.

[13] B. van Iersel, "The Finding of Jesus in the Temple. Some Observations on the Original Form of Luke ii 41-51a," *Novum Testamentum* 4 (1960) 169–70.

[14] For example, John Nolland, *Luke 1–9:20* (Dallas: Word Books, 1989) 134.

[15] Joseph A. Fitzmyer, *The Gospel according to Luke* (I–IX) (New York: Doubleday, 1981) 443.

[16] B. Perrin, *Plutarch's Lives.* IX *Demetrius and Antony.* Loeb Classical Library (London: Heinemann, 1920) 193.

[17] Scott S. Bartchy, "Slavery" in *Anchor Bible Dictionary* (New York: Doubleday, 1992) 6:67.

[18] Dale Martin, *Slavery as Salvation: The Metaphor of Slavery in Pauline Christianity* (New Haven, CT: Yale University Press, 1990) 48.

[19] Acts 22:27-28; Martin, *Slavery as Salvation,* 32.

[20] Jennifer Glancy, *Slavery in Early Christianity* (Oxford: Oxford University Press, 2002) 17.

[21] Martin, *Slavery as Salvation,* 2–7.

[22] W. Miller, *Cicero. De Officiis.* Loeb Classical Library (London: Heinemann, 1921) 153–55.

[23] H.-I. Marrou, *Histoire de l'éducation dans l'antiquité* (Paris: Seuil, 1948) 200–22.

[24] Martin Hengel, *Judaism and Hellenism. Studies in Their Encounter in Palestine in the Early Hellenistic Period* (Philadelphia: Fortress Press, 1974) 1:75.

[25] Marrou, *Histoire de l'éducation dans l'antiquité*, 214.

[26] Ibid., 240.

[27] Ibid., 269.

[28] Jeffrey R. Asher, *Polarity and Change in 1 Corinthians 15. A Study of Metaphysics, Rhetoric and Resurrection* (Tübingen: Mohr Siebeck, 2000).

[29] Thomas Schmeller, "Stoics, Stoicism," in *Anchor Bible Dictionary* (New York: Doubleday, 1992) 6:213.

[30] H. L. Jones, *The Geography of Strabo.* Loeb Classical Library (London: Heinemann, 1949) 347.

Chapter 4

Temporary Vocations as Prophet and Pharisee: Commitment to the Law

In their quest for an identity and purpose in life Jesus and Paul moved out of the environments in which they had been brought up. They traveled to strange places where they knew no one. There they underwent a first conversion that was to determine their lifestyles for years to come, perhaps only one or two years for Jesus, closer to fifteen years in the case of Paul. In both cases, they were totally and passionately committed, on occasion to the point where their actions revealed them to be "zealots." They lived on charity. Subsequently, in midlife, each was to undergo a second conversion that meant another radical change in the way they saw themselves and their mission.

Jesus

Mark records the event in just one sentence. "In those days Jesus came from Nazareth of Galilee and was baptized by John in the Jordan" (1:9). The year was probably between 24 and 26 c.e.[1] We do not know when John the Baptist began his mission, but in all probability it was not much earlier. Jesus would have responded immediately to the news of a new prophet, a potential source of enlightenment. His family and the doctors of the law (Luke 2:41-51) having failed him, Jesus was living on a knife edge of anxiety, eager for any hint that might show him what God required of him. And that stressful condition had now gone on for over twenty years.

The intensity of Jesus' expectation, and the extent to which it interfered with normal life, is underlined by the fact that he had not married, even though it was a matter of obligation for Jews (Gen 1:28). This was not because of any commitment to celibacy, but because he wanted to be entirely without ties in order to respond with total freedom when God's call came to him.

The historicity of Jesus' baptism by John is universally accepted, but there has been much discussion of what Jesus thought he was doing in submitting to a baptism signifying repentance for sin.[2] From the perspective adopted in this study, he accepted John's God-given message in all its dimensions, which would not have presented any difficulty, with a view to showing John that he was worthy of a considered response to questions regarding his destiny.

We have no idea of what passed between Jesus and John, but a significant inference can be made from Jesus' subsequent behavior. Prior to his baptism, as far as we know, he had been an artisan in Nazareth or in one of the little towns around the lake, where repairs to wooden boats would have supplemented income from farm and domestic objects. After his baptism, as we shall see in detail in a moment, he appears as a wandering preacher whose message is the same as that of John. The Baptist, therefore, must have convinced Jesus that it was his vocation to be a prophet. On what possible basis could John, alone or in dialogue with Jesus, have come to this conclusion?

The Vocation of Prophet

Had Jesus explained the virgin birth, as he must have done in order to justify the urgency of his question, the closest explicative analogy that would instinctively occur to John was the passage of the Scriptures in which God said to Jeremiah, "Before I formed you in the belly I knew you, and before you came out of the womb I consecrated you; I appointed you as a prophet to the nations" (1:5). "Before I formed you in the belly" and "before you came out of the womb" are an example of synonymous parallelism. The same moment in time is indicated in two slightly different ways. Clearly, therefore, the reference is not to conception but to the growth of the embryo in the womb. After Jeremiah it became a common belief that the young child in its mother's womb is formed by God as proof of his loving care (e.g., Ps 139:13; Job 10:8-9). This, perhaps, might explain why Jesus had not found the text of Jeremiah applicable to his situation. There was no real parallel to the idea of direct divine causality in conception.

However, the verb translated here by "to form" is *yatsar,* which had acquired the technical meaning of "to create" from its use in Genesis 2:7-8, and which is in fact used in this sense elsewhere in Jeremiah (51:19). Thus, it is not at all surprising that the Targum of Jeremiah, whose origins can be dated to Palestine during, or slightly before, the first century C.E.,[3] should have substituted *bara* for *yatsar.*[4] The translation thus runs, "Before I created you from the womb I established you, and before you came into the world I appointed you."[5] The appearance of *bara* would immediately have reminded everyone that it is the very first verb to appear in the Bible, "In the beginning God created *(bara)* the heavens and the earth" (Gen 1:1). When read against this background of the might of God's creative activity, it would be easy to think there was no place for the intervention of a husband in Jeremiah 1:4. From this perspective, therefore, it provided a clear response to Jesus' question. If God had "created" Jeremiah to be a prophet, then it seemed highly probable that this was also his intention for Jesus, whom he had "created in the womb" of Mary.

If Jesus was to be a prophet like Jeremiah, what should his message be? The basic concern of all the prophets was the reform of the Jewish people, and that call to repentance was being articulated here and now by John the Baptist. The obvious thing for Jesus to do was to join forces with John, and that is precisely what happened. Whatever plans Jesus had to return to Galilee were set aside. It was only after the arrest of John that he went back to his adopted homeland (Mark 1:14).

At the time when Jesus joined him, John was based on the east bank of the lower Jordan valley across from Jericho. This is the inescapable conclusion from a series of convergent indications in the Gospels. He preached in "the wilderness of Judea" (Matt 3:1), but those who accepted his message were subsequently baptized "in the river Jordan" (Matt 3:6). Hence, it must have been a lonely area immediately adjacent to the river.

But which side? The Fourth Gospel is the only one to answer this question. It tells us that the Jerusalem authorities interrogated the Baptist "in Bethany beyond the Jordan" (John 1:28). In itself the phrase "beyond the Jordan" (that also appears in John 3:26 and 10:40) is ambiguous, because it depends on where one is standing. It is most probable, however, that in all three cases the evangelist is speaking from the perspective of a Jerusalemite, i.e., a west-banker. The need to specify that the Bethany in question was on the east bank of the Jordan arose because the evangelist knew of a Bethany on the west bank, namely "Bethany near Jerusalem" (John 11:18).

This interpretation is confirmed by the fact that much later, when Jesus was in danger of arrest in Roman-controlled Judea (John 10:39; 11:7), and had to flee to another jurisdiction, "he went away again across the Jordan to the place where John at first baptized" (John 10:40). The east bank of the Jordan, known as Peraea, was attached to the kingdom of Galilee ruled by Herod Antipas. Neither the writ of Rome nor that of its puppet religious leaders in Jerusalem ran there.

The importance of "again" and "at first" in John 10:40 is not always appreciated. The former implies that Jesus had been there before. The natural interpretation is that this is where he first met John and was baptized by him. "At first," however, reveals that the Jordan was only the earliest place at which John baptized. Do we know where else? This question is answered most explicitly by a passage in the Fourth Gospel that must be accepted as authentic:[6]

> After this Jesus and his disciples went into the land of Judea, and there he remained with them and was baptizing. John also was baptizing at Aenon near Salim, because there was much water there. And people came and were baptized, because John had not yet been put into prison. (John 3:22-24)

Jesus is here depicted as having left Peraea to exercise a baptizing mission identical to that of John, but in Judea where the terrain had already been prepared by the Baptist, who had preached to Jerusalemites and Judeans (Mark 1:5; Matt 3:5). John shows his leadership in choosing the more difficult mission territory. Aenon ("Springs") is to be identified with the five springs on the east slope of Mount Gerizim facing the still-existent village of Salim some 4.5 kilometers out in the plain to the east.[7] John had gone into the heartland of the Samaritans for whom Mount Gerizim was the holy mountain (John 4:5 and 20). John, however, had little success among the hostile Samaritans, and eventually left for Galilee, where his criticism of the king's marriage led to his arrest and eventual execution (Mark 6:17-29).

Zeal for the Law

Where did Jesus minister in Judea? Given the urgency of the reforming message, "even now (= already) the axe is laid to the root of the trees" (Matt 3:10), no doubt John and Jesus had worked out the strategy of their two-pronged mission before leaving Peraea. If John headed straight for the Samaritan heartland, then it is extremely unlikely Jesus spent time in Jericho. Its inhabitants had had plenty of opportunities to hear the Baptist. It is barely an hour's walk from Jericho to the ford in the Jordan where John baptized. Moreover, there are no towns or villages on the road between Jericho and Jerusalem, and the character of the terrain made it impracticable to strike northwest or southwest of that road. Thus, if Jesus was not to waste time in the countryside, he can only have gone due west to the Holy City.

Jerusalem was the place where he would reach the greatest number of Jews, and the obvious place to encounter them was the Temple. It served both religious and secular needs. When Jesus went there, work was still being done on the structures erected by Herod the Great. He had doubled the size of the original much-repaired Temple, which meant that the traditional religious area had to be separated from the extension where pagans were welcomed and business took place. A wall, therefore, separated the sanctuary *(naos)* in the center from the Temple precincts *(hieron)*, namely, the Court of the Gentiles, whose principal building was the great basilica along the south wall. It was the civic center of the city.

It is to this missionary expedition that we must date the cleansing of the Temple.

> (13) The Passover of the Jews was at hand, and Jesus went up to Jerusalem. (14) In the temple precincts he found people selling oxen and sheep and pigeons, and the money-changers at their business. (15) So he made a kind of lash out of cords, and drove the whole pack of them out of the temple precincts with their sheep and oxen. And he overturned the tables of the money-changers, spilling their coins. (16) And he told those who sold the pigeons, "Get these things out of here. You shall not make my Father's house a house of trade." (17) His disciples remember that it was written, "Zeal for your house will consume me." (Ps 69:10) (John 2:13-17)

This story is not without its problems. The moneychangers can plausibly be located in the basilica at the south end of Herod's vast enclosure. The animals and birds for sale as sacrificial victims must have been at the opposite end; the north wall of the Temple had the only gate communicating with the open countryside (John 5:2; *m. Middoth* 1.3). How could Jesus get away with disturbances at two such widely separated parts of the Temple? Why did the Temple police not intervene at the first and so block the second? Moreover, it is inconceivable that one man could expel the hundreds of people in the basilica, or that a single individual could herd a mass of frightened animals. All of this, however, is but an example of the condensation and hyperbole integral to a good story. If they are set aside, it is easy to extract a plausible core. Jesus tried to herd out some of those buying and selling, and turned over one or two tables of the moneychangers. There was no big fuss and it was all over quickly. Instinctively the bystanders would have recognized that Jesus was not running amuck, but making a considered gesture. In all probability many would have sympathized.

The fouling of the esplanade by the droppings of animals would have been offensive to many, but that was not a religious issue. The role played by the moneychangers was another matter. To many they were the visible facade of a corrupt system that was in blatant violation of the Law.

The money for the Temple tax had to pass through the hands of the moneychangers. The purpose of this tax was to permit all Israelite males, wherever they were in the world, to participate in the daily whole-offering that atoned for sins of the people. The amount of the tax was a half-shekel, and it had to be paid each year in the coinage of Tyre (*m. Bekhoroth* 8:7).

The first problem was the frequency of the tax. That it had to be paid yearly was a tradition reaching back several hundred years (Neh 10:32; 2 Chr 24:5), yet, according to Exodus 30:11-16, the original legislation, it would appear that it was to be paid only once in a lifetime. This was certainly the interpretation in force among the strictly observant Essenes at Qumran (4Q159, frag. 1, col. 2, lines 6-7), and was one of the points of dispute they had with the Temple authorities.

The second problem was the prescribed coinage. Far from being the transfer of "secular" coins bearing pagan royal images into aniconic "holy" coins, as commentators regularly assume,[8] the service provided by the moneychangers in the Temple was to make available to Jews the Tyrian coinage the Temple authorities demanded. The shekel of Tyre, however, bore two images. On the obverse was the head of the god Melkart (or Herakles), and on the reverse an eagle. In other words, pious Jews, who brought legal aniconic Jewish coinage to pay their tax, were obliged in the Temple to exchange it for coins bearing the image of a false god.[9] In their holiest place Jews were being forced to handle and look upon idols—to many the equivalent of committing idolatry.

Apart from the one text from Qumran (4Q159), there is no evidence of any popular outcry against these two abuses. The regulations had been in force for so long they were taken for granted. Only an extreme legal purist could possibly be overtly critical. Jesus, however, did object publicly by means of a prophetic gesture, in principle directed against the Temple authorities, but that in practice hit those most easily accessible, the moneychangers, who of course were not responsible for policy. Today riot police often bear the burden of anger inspired by their government.

The disciples of Jesus saw his action in the Temple as evidence of his "zeal" (v. 17). In fact, his violent action marked him out as a "zealot," not in the sense of a member of the violent revolutionary group that came into being much later in Jerusalem in the winter of 67–8 c.e., but in the much older individual sense of "a Jew who was intensely zealous for the practice of the Mosaic Law and insistent that his fellow Jews strictly observe the Law as a means of distinguishing and separating Israel, God's holy people, from the idolatry and immorality practiced by neighbouring Gentiles."[10] Such Jews were animated by an intense personal conviction that sometimes led them to punish faithless Jews (Elijah in Sir 48:1-2) or even to murder them (Phinehas in Num 25:6-8; Mattathias in 1 Macc 2:23-24). Admiration for their acts rang down the centuries (Philo, *Spec. Leg.* 2.253), and passed into enabling legislation (*m. Sanhedrin* 9.6).

No such violence is attested for John the Baptist. In the case of Jesus we can detect the intense legalism of a new convert. On previous visits to the Temple, he no doubt accepted what everyone else did. On this occasion he wore the mantle of a prophet for the first time, and saw what went on in the Temple with new eyes. His zeal was inflamed by his sense of outrage that the Jewish authorities had not only distorted the law of God, but had invited a foreign god into the holiest place in Judaism.

This episode in the life of Jesus has its parallel in that of Paul. When he was living his temporary vocation as a Pharisee, he saw his violent attack on Christians as proof of his "zeal" for the Law (Gal 1:14-15; Phil 3:6).

The two texts, the finding in the Temple (Luke 2:41-51) and the cleansing of the Temple (John 2:13-17), are linked by a reference on the lips of Jesus to his "Father's house." These are the only NT texts that speak of the Temple in this way. This shared element serves to highlight the change that has taken place in Jesus. Once, as a child, he had hoped to find enlightenment in the Temple. Now, as a prophet, it was his responsibility to purify it.

Jesus Returns to Galilee

How long Jesus stayed in Jerusalem we do not know. His return to Galilee is dated by the arrest of John the Baptist (Mark 1:14). The motive of the latter's detention was his criticism of the marriage of Antipas with Herodias, the wife of his half-brother Philip (Mark 6:17). The latest possible date for this marriage was 23 c.e.[11] In contrast to Jesus' success in Judea (John 3:26), John failed in Samaria (John 4:1), where a Jewish prophet would be given little welcome. The hatred of Samaritans for Jews was fully reciprocated. The point of the parable of the Good Samaritan (Luke 10:30-37) was to force a Jew to admit that a Samaritan could be "good." John took a considerable risk (Luke 9:51-56) in order to leave Judea free for Jesus. The only mission field left to the Baptist was Galilee where there were large numbers of Jews. There was no reason for him to go back to Peraea, and it was only in one or other of these regions that he could have been arrested by Antipas.

Once John had been taken out of circulation, one of his disciples brought the news to Jesus, because the situation could be very serious. At that time no one was condemned to prison as a punishment. Those confined were either under investigation (there was no bail) or awaiting execution. At first Jesus could not have known John's situation. As long as he was being held in Galilee, probably in the new capital, Tiberias, there was some hope. Jesus became seriously worried only when he learned that John had been transferred to the remote desert fortress of Machaerus in Peraea.

This made it imperative to maintain the momentum of the Baptist's mission in Galilee, and Jesus made the decision to move there to fill John's place. He was now the de facto leader of the Baptist reforming movement. How seriously he took the responsibility is clear from the fact that he cannot have been ignorant that his going to Galilee was putting himself in danger. Like every ruler in the region, and notably his father, Antipas had an efficient network of spies and informers. From the moment they began to attract followers, John and Jesus would have been marked men. They might be planning a rebellion. In fact, according to Josephus, Antipas interpreted John's message in political terms (AJ 18.118). Jesus would have been watched from the moment he stepped over the border, because he was identified with the Baptist. Mark's account is closest to the event:

> (14) And King Herod heard, for Jesus' name had become known, and some said, "John the Baptizer has been raised from the dead; that is why these powers are at work in him." (15) But others said, "It is Elijah." And others said, "It is a prophet, like one of the prophets." (16) Hearing, Herod said, "John, whom I beheaded, has been raised." (Mark 6:14-16)

There is an unusual amount of verbal repetition in this short and rather confused story. That Herod "heard" is mentioned twice, as is the "raising" of John from the dead. This sort of thing usually means that a story has been retouched by an editor. If his addition is set aside, the original source reads, "Herod heard, for Jesus' name had become known, and said, 'John whom I beheaded has been raised.'"

If, in Mark's source, Jesus was thought to be the resurrected John, it can only be because Jesus was saying and doing what the Baptist had said and done in Galilee. As Jesus had done in Judea, he was now doing in Galilee, proclaiming a baptism of repentance for the remission of sins. Jesus, therefore, appeared in Galilee as a prophet of the same stamp as John the Baptist. Jesus' baptizing mission in Galilee, however, did not last long. At some point there was a second conversion, parallel to Paul's experience on the road to Damascus, because the pattern of Jesus' activity changed. He ceased to baptize, and his message was no longer "Repent!" but "Follow me!" Acceptance of his teaching on the kingdom of God replaced obedience to the Law as the touchstone of salvation.

Paul

The Jerusalem that Paul found at the end of his eight-hundred-kilometer, six-week march from Tarsus, probably in the company of a group of Passover pilgrims, was luminous with the golden stone of buildings that were not much older than he was. His heavy Roman catapults having pounded the city for fifty-five days in 37 B.C.E., Herod the Great inherited a wasteland, but his energy and powers of organization rebuilt it with a magnificence that challenged the great cities of the Orient.

Only when the feast had ended did Paul have time to consider his future. He tells us that he joined the sect of the Pharisees (Phil 3:5). Luke makes this seem very natural because he has Paul say "I am a Pharisee, a son of Pharisees" (Acts 23:6). In other words, Paul made no deliberate option about his future, but merely accepted without conscious decision the religious option of his parents.

It is most improbable that Luke is correct in this. The Pharisees were an urban phenomenon limited to Jerusalem. Paul's parents might have encountered Pharisees in Galilee, where they came on brief visits to inspect the tithing and quality of produce being sent to Jerusalem. But there was no local branch of the Pharisees in Gischala, whose inhabitants would have been dismissed as "the common people" from whom the Pharisees carefully distinguished themselves. Nor were there any Pharisees in the diaspora, so Paul's parents could not have joined the sect in Tarsus. Hence, if Paul became a Pharisee it was his personal decision, and it must have been made in Jerusalem. The importance of his choice, however, must not be exaggerated. He did not have many options.

Josephus tells us that in addition to the hereditary priesthood, to which only blood gave admission, there were four major groupings among Jews: the Pharisees, the Sadducees, the Essenes, and the Zealots (AJ 18.11-25).

The last mentioned, in the sense that Josephus intended, can be dismissed at once. They did not yet exist as an organized revolutionary group when Paul arrived in Jerusalem around 15 c.e. The high-principled Essenes might have appeared attractive to an idealistic young man, but one who had learned tolerance in the diaspora would have been appalled at the arrogant belief of the Essenes that they alone of all Jews possessed the truth. Moreover, he would not normally have encountered them in Jerusalem. They had marginalized themselves even physically by living in villages and in remote desert settlements like Qumran.

The Sadducees, on the contrary, were a mainstream group whose authority far exceeded their numbers.[12] They were aristocrats of wealth and/or power. Their members belonged to the great priestly families that ruled the country in the absence of Jewish kings, and to the rich landed class of laity who allied themselves with them. Inevitably they were surrounded by clients and hangers on who hoped to benefit from the crumbs that dropped from the tables of power.

Herod the Great had sidelined the Sadducees, but they regained power when the Romans assumed direct control of Palestine in 6 c.e. The high priest and his allies were responsible for the day-to-day management of the country. Their exercise of political power inevitably tended to give practical expediency greater importance than religious principles. Discrepancies between theory and practice, which might give the impression of laxity, were dismissed autocratically. Discussion was not welcomed. The Sadducees knew perfectly well that they did not have to be liked, and were quite sure that they had the means to ensure that they were respected. Their leadership style did not require their behavior to excite admiration, or their orders to be so presented as to persuade. Like all conservative groups they simplified their life by adherence to a code that was interpreted literally and strictly. The complexities of jurisprudence that had developed since the Exile were thus simply swept aside as not written in the Law of Moses.

It would have been immediately obvious to Paul that he did not have the resources to break into this aloof, cold, patrician class. As an exclusive hereditary group, they might have welcomed into their midst an extremely wealthy Jew from the diaspora, because they would have had much in common. A young man barely out of his teens had nothing to contribute to them, and all they had to offer him was the humiliating status of a client.

The Pharisees

The Pharisees would have judged Paul differently.[13] He would have been a welcome recruit. As a well-educated diaspora Jew, he might lack detailed knowledge of the content of the Law, but he had the intellectual training to appreciate their concern for the precise interpretation of legal norms, and the dialectical ability to pursue truth in dialogue. He also had the cultural depth to value their respect for "the traditions of the fathers," the body of customary legal interpretation, conserved in memory through constant repetition, to which the Pharisees gave the same normative value as the written legislation of the Scriptures.

Given their mission, the Pharisees were recruited from the literate stratum of the population below the aristocratic class, namely, teachers, bureaucrats, functionaries. They had an agenda for the people in that they had a vision of a new religious and social identity for Jews in a swiftly changing world. They could not impose their vision because they had no access to the levers of power so firmly grasped by the Sadducees. Yet the latter had to deal with them carefully. The Pharisees were the ones who made the day-to-day business of government function. They could make life hard or easy for their masters, who were always looking over their shoulders at the Roman overlord. They could oil the bearings or put sand in the gears, and Rome would not tolerate any disruption of public order. The Pharisees could not be ignored by the Sadducees.

The Pharisees enjoyed great popularity among the people. They were respected for their learning, and admired for their observance. They were not seen as nit-picking legalists because they made no effort to impose their opinions. On the contrary, they were appreciated as experts who could give a clear answer to questions regarding the requirements of the Law in matters of daily domestic life. Over two-thirds of their surviving teachings deal with dietary laws, ritual purity for meals, and the quality and tithing of agricultural produce.

Paul's time in Jerusalem coincided with the prime of the great Pharisaic teacher Gamaliel I, who was celebrated for his wise tolerance (Acts 5:34). An enthusiastic recruit like Paul would have eagerly sought his guidance (Acts 22:3) because from day one it would have been drilled into him that "an ignorant man cannot be holy" (*m. Aboth* 2.6).[14] The mild Hillel went so far as to say, "he who does not learn is worthy of death" (*m. Aboth* 1.13).[15]

Legislation is clarified by common study and discussion. Thus the Pharisees spent considerable time debating each other. This tendency to congregate was reinforced by the recognition that life was greatly simplified if one ate with those who obeyed the same highly exigent dietary laws. Then one did not have to wonder if this or that requirement had been met. Only with like-minded "companions" could they be fully themselves in freedom. Table fellowship, in consequence, was the high point of Pharisaic group activity.

It takes little experience to imagine the hothouse atmosphere of such groups, particularly if they contained a high proportion of young men. It would have stimulated all their competitive drives. When holier-than-thou was conditioned by smarter-than-thou, exhibitionistic excesses were inevitable. Arrogance bred contempt for those slower or less insightful. Fine distinctions were pushed to the extreme, where mere hair-splitting appeared to be an appropriate occupation for a butcher with a cleaver. Ever increasing refinement moved the students ever further from reality. The feverish atmosphere of incessant debate is graphically evoked by the sad words of Simeon, the son of Gamaliel I, after he had acquired wisdom, "All my days I have grown up among the Sages and I have found nothing better for a person than silence. The expounding of the Law is not the chief thing, but the doing of it, and he that multiplies words occasions sin" (*m. Aboth* 1.17).[16]

Paul was not immune. In fact he participated fully. Writing many years later, and looking back at a period in his life he had completely rejected, he still could not keep a note of smug self-satisfaction out of his words: "I was advancing in Judaism beyond many Jews of my own age, so extremely zealous was I for the traditions of my fathers" (Gal 1:14). He had fought and he had won! His achievement is undeniable. Gamaliel I probably formally introduced his son Simeon to Pharisaic jurisprudence at the age of ten (*m. Aboth* 5.21).[17] Paul did not start until he was about twenty. Just one example will illustrate how much he had to make up. The law concerning the Sabbath forbade thirty-nine different types of work (*m. Shabbath* 7.2),[18] each with multiple subdivisions. Even the rabbis were forced to confess with wry humor, "the rules about the Sabbath are as mountains hanging by a hair, for the teaching of Scripture thereon is scanty and the rules many" (*m. Hagigah* 1.8).[19]

The energy and total dedication implied in his claim to have caught up successfully meant that Paul had studied full time. As Ben Sira said with great common sense, "the wisdom of the scribe depends on leisure; only the one who has little business can become wise"; thus "no artisan or master craftsman who labors by night as well as by day" can be a scholar (Sir 38:24-27). Any occupation was a distraction from study. Not surprisingly, therefore, there is no evidence that rabbis worked at trades prior to the destruction of Jerusalem in 70 C.E. Thereafter, when there was no longer any institutionalized charity in the ruined city, necessity was transformed into a virtue: "All study of the Law without worldly labor comes to naught at the last and brings sin in its train" (*m. Aboth* 2.2).[20]

Charity and Love

If Paul had to be supported during his studies, who paid? Possibly his family. If they had the resources to give him an expensive education in Tarsus, they could have continued to pay for him in Jerusalem. Another possibility is that those Pharisees who earned salaries as government functionaries subsidized full-time students, as happens in some Ultra Orthodox Jewish communities today. Even if they did not, there was a substitute mechanism in place. An obscure law, which may never have been enforced, stipulated that every Israelite had to spend part of his income in Jerusalem. This was designed to supplement the charitable funds pilgrims to the Temple were required to bring. Without this there would have been chaos because "Jerusalem had already in Jesus' time become a city of idlers, and the considerable proletariat living on the religious importance of the city was one of its most outstanding peculiarities."[21]

Despite their poverty, no Pharisee refused marriage as a means of economizing. Like all Jews they understood "Be fruitful and multiply" (Gen 1:28) as a binding precept. As an immigrant from the diaspora who desperately wanted to be accepted, there can be little doubt that Paul cheerfully bowed to the expectation that young men would be married in their twenties. He could not have spoken so complacently about his success in Galatians 1:14 had he been pertinaciously disobedient to a fundamental social obligation.

In this respect, Paul's young manhood was radically different from that of Jesus, who postponed everything as he waited for God's call.

When Jesus did finally discover his true vocation, he remained single. Similarly, Paul was single when he was active as a Christian missionary (1 Cor 7:8; cf. 9:5). What had happened to his wife and children? His complete silence would suggest an event so traumatic, e.g., death in childbirth or an accident, that the memory was too painful to be revisited and too sacred to be disclosed to others.

Overlap in Jerusalem

It is another coincidence that Paul and Jesus were in Jerusalem at the same time. The duration of Paul's stay as a Pharisee can be established with a relatively high degree of precision, namely, from his arrival around 15 c.e. until his conversion probably about 33 c.e. As regards Jesus, it is certain that he was crucified in Jerusalem on 7 April 30 c.e. It would appear from the Fourth Gospel that he spent the greater part of his two-year (?) ministry there[22] in addition to the time he spent in the Holy City as a disciple of John the Baptist.

There is no hint of this overlap, either in the Gospel tradition or the letters of Paul. Such silence, of course, is not an objection. Paul's total commitment to his studies ruled out curiosity regarding anything extraneous. This Pharisaic attitude still exists. Modern rabbinical students in Jerusalem were completely unaware of the extraordinary peace-making visit of Anwar Sadat, the president of Egypt, on 19 November 1977.

Equally, it should not be assumed that Jesus made a significant impact in Jerusalem either as a disciple of John the Baptist or later. Success generates excitement and notoriety. Failure does not. With the possible exception of Nicodemus (John 7:52), we do not know of a single convert Jesus made in Jerusalem. Not surprisingly, the Synoptics give pride of place to Galilee where he had some success at least. Even the crucifixion of Jesus would not have caused a stir because it occurred on the busiest day in the year, the eve of Passover—that year on a Friday—which meant that all preparations for the meal had to be finished by sunset.

Zeal for the Law

Paul became interested in Jesus only when he saw the movement that claimed allegiance to him gaining in numbers. The Pharisees would have reacted immediately to what they perceived as a threat to their monopoly of popular opinion. Recruits to another flag were lost to theirs. The Christians were fortunate that Paul's teacher, the influential Gamaliel I, advised a wait-and-see attitude:

In the present case I tell you, keep away from these men, and let them alone. For if this plan or this undertaking is of men, it will fail. But if it is of God, you will not be able to overthrow them. You might even be found opposing God. (Acts 5:38-39)

Clearly Gamaliel did not consider the "Messianists" (AJ 18.64) as something new and dangerous. Jesus was not the first misguided individual to think he was the Messiah, and if his followers were ignored they would quietly fade away. This assessment would have found support in the fact that Christians were not disturbing the social order. Whatever they thought about the Messiah, they lived as good Jews, and continued to frequent the Temple without interrupting the worship (Acts 2:46). Judaism was very tolerant of deviant ideas provided they did not threaten social cohesion.

For Paul, however, that was precisely the danger of the proclamation of Jesus as the Messiah. Temperamentally, he was impatient with a wait-and-see approach to anything, particularly when, as he saw it, the menace was grave and growing. He was amazed that the Christians themselves apparently understood their situation as a comfortable "both-and" in which they could have the best of both worlds. It should have been obvious to everyone that it was an "either-or" moment that permitted of no equivocation. A supremely important choice had to be made. It was not possible to sit on the fence and pretend there was no problem.

Like all Jews, Paul saw the Law and the Messiah in a sequential relationship. The here and now was the period of the Law. Sometime in the unforeseeable future the Messiah would arrive, and the world would change. He would bring all blessings, and there would be joy and gladness, untroubled by war, discord, or strife. Above all, the people of the Messiah would be free from sin. "In his days there shall be no wickedness in their midst, for all shall be holy" (*Psalms of Solomon* 17:32; cf. Isa 60:21; Ezek 36:25; Sir 24:22; 1 Enoch 5:8-9). Thus, there was no necessity for the Law, because "the law is laid down not for the just but for the lawless and disobedient, for the unholy and profane" (1 Tim 1:9). In a perfect world law is completely irrelevant. The Law, however, was so integral to Judaism that an idyllic future without the Law was emotionally unacceptable. Inevitably various speculative efforts were made to assign the Law a role in the Messianic age.[23] Paul's incisive intelligence rejected the inherent contradiction of this view. It had to be either the Law or the Messiah. Thus he saw the proclamation of Jesus of Nazareth as the Christ, the Messianic Savior, as condemnation of the Law.

Christians were in effect saying that the Law was no longer relevant or necessary. For several reasons they could not possibly be right. First, Jesus Christ did not in any way resemble the Messiah that Paul as a Pharisee expected. The Pharisaic *Psalms of Solomon* depicted a warrior king who would purge Jerusalem of Gentiles and expel all aliens from the land (*PsSol* 17 and 18). Second, not only had the world not changed for the better, it had not changed at all. From Paul's perspective, therefore, Jesus of Nazareth had led his followers astray. He was now unfortunately beyond Paul's reach, but his followers needed correction. They had to be brought back to the truth, to a lifestyle in which the Law reigned supreme. If Paul was the only Pharisee to see this problem, it was up to him to do something about it.

Contrary to what Luke tells us, Paul had no authority to arrest or punish the followers of Jesus. Nor is there any hint that he took the law into his own hands. This is suggested by some translations of *kath' hyperbolên* in Galatians 1:13, e.g., "violently" (RSV, NRSV), "savagely" (NEB), "simply no limit" (NJB), "to extremes" (NAB), but the context and Paul's usage elsewhere show that the adverb expresses the quality of his commitment ("intensely"), not the means he employed. He was completely dedicated to, and totally involved in, what became for him a habitual activity.

Christianity brought to life a new dimension of the zeal that had always burned in Paul's heart. The hostility with which he attempted to drive Christians back to the Law made him a "zealot" in the old classical sense, and clearly he was proud to stand in that tradition (Gal 1:13-14; Phil 3:5). Words were his weapons, confrontation his strategy, and verbal harassment his tactic. He would never rest, and was determined to grind down the followers of Jesus. He could challenge, revile, insult, slander, threaten—in a word, make the lives of Christians a misery. He could try to make them blaspheme (Acts 26:11) by demanding public assent to formulations that effectively denied Jesus, e.g., to an oath or a prayer implying that the Messiah had not yet come. If he attacked Christians publicly in the synagogue on Shabbat, the pressure he could bring to bear was considerable.

According to Luke, Paul left Jerusalem bearing letters from the high priest "to the synagogues at Damascus, so that if he found any belonging to the Way, men or women, he might bring them bound to Jerusalem" (Acts 9:2). This scenario is completely implausible. The authority of the high priest extended only to Jerusalem and the eleven toparchies that surrounded it. His writ did not run in Galilee, and certainly not in the

Roman province of Syria to which Damascus belonged. The governor would have given short shrift to anyone who attempted to abduct individuals under the protection of Rome.

Nonetheless, it was in the vicinity of Damascus that Paul encountered the risen Lord. If this chapter began with two journeys, it also ends with two journeys. This time both start from Jerusalem and head northward. Jesus went to Galilee, and Paul to Damascus. We know that Jesus moved in order to take the place of John the Baptist. We do not know why Paul was on the road to Damascus. Many guesses have been made. The simplest is that he was on the way to visit his parents in Tarsus. For security, the sensible thing would have been to join one of the frequent caravans from Jerusalem to Damascus, a great trading crossroad, and then another heading west to Anatolia. The journeys of both Jesus and Paul ended in a second conversion.

Notes

[1] Christiane Saulnier, "Hérode Antipas et Jean le Baptiste. Quelques remarques sur les confusions chronologiques de Flavius Josèphe," *Revue Biblique* 91 (1984) 375.

[2] W. D. Davies and Dale Allison, *A Critical and Exegetical Commentary on the Gospel of Matthew*. I. *Chs. 1–7*, International Critical Commentary (Edinburgh: Clark, 1988) 321–23.

[3] Robert Hayward, *The Targum of Jeremiah*, The Aramaic Bible, vol. 12 (Wilmington, DE: Michael Glazier, 1986) 38.

[4] Alexander Sperber, *The Bible in Aramaic*. III. *The Latter Prophets According to Targum Jonathan* (Leiden: Brill, 1962) 133.

[5] Hayward, *The Targum of Jeremiah*, 46.

[6] Joachim Jeremias, *New Testament Theology*. I. *The Proclamation of Jesus* (London: SCM Press, 1971) 45–46.

[7] Jerome Murphy-O'Connor, "John the Baptist and Jesus: History and Hypotheses," *New Testament Studies* 36 (1990) 362–66.

[8] For example, E. P. Sanders, *Jesus and Judaism* (Philadelphia: Fortress, 1985) 64.

[9] Peter Richardson, "Why Turn the Tables? Jesus' Protest in the Temple Precincts," *Society of Biblical Literature 1992 Seminar Papers*, no. 31, ed. E. H. Lovering (Atlanta: Scholars, 1992) 507–23.

[10] John P. Meier, *A Marginal Jew. Rethinking the Historical Jesus*. III. *Companions and Competitors* (New York: Doubleday, 2001) 206.

[11] Saulnier, "Hérode Antipas et Jean le Baptiste. Quelques remarques sur les confusions chronologiques de Flavius Josèphe," 375.

[12] Meier, *A Marginal Jew. Rethinking the Historical Jesus*. III. *Companions and Competitors*, 389–410.

[13] Ibid., 313–32.

[14] H. Danby, *The Mishnah* (Oxford: Oxford University Press, 1993) 448.

[15] Ibid., 447.

[16] Ibid., 447.

[17] Ibid., 458.

[18] Ibid., 106.

[19] Ibid., 212.

[20] Ibid., 447.

[21] Joachim Jeremias, *Jerusalem in the Time of Jesus. An Investigation into Economic and Social Conditions during the New Testament Period* (London: SCM Press, 1969) 118.

[22] C. H. Dodd, *Historical Tradition in the Fourth Gospel* (Cambridge: Cambridge University Press, 1963) 243–47.

[23] W. D. Davies, *Torah in the Messianic Age and/or the Age to Come,* Journal of Biblical Literature Monograph Series 7 (Philadelphia: Society of Biblical Literature, 1952) 47–48.

Chapter 5

A Second Conversion: Rejection of the Law

The journeys Jesus and Paul undertook in the course of what we now know to be their temporary vocations brought them to destinations they never anticipated. Jesus' conversion may not have been as instantaneous as that of Paul, but both were changed radically. The Jesus who left Galilee for his last visit to Jerusalem thought of himself in a completely different way to his self-understanding as a disciple of John the Baptist. When Paul reached Damascus he was no longer a zealous Pharisee. Each underwent a second conversion that was to determine the definitive direction of their lives. Both made a decision that would ultimately be the cause of their deaths.

Jesus

The Jesus who emerges from the pages of the Gospels is clearly not a deputy prophet, a disciple of John the Baptist. This is made evident in a variety of ways, but two are of great importance. Jesus compares and contrasts himself with the Baptist to the ultimate detriment of John. He presents himself as no longer John's disciple but as his superior. Closely bound up with this is a complete turnabout in Jesus' attitude toward the Law. All the prophets thought of themselves as the servants of the Law, whose demands they interpreted strictly and discharged as perfectly as possible. Jesus, on the contrary, sets himself above the Law. He refuses to bow to its requirements. It does not dominate or control his life.

Jesus and John the Baptist

The relationship of Jesus and the Baptist was an issue of great concern to the early church, and in order to clarify the problem Q brought together three blocks of material in which Jesus addressed the issue, in all likelihood at different times. That Jesus actually said the words that follow emerges with great probability from the detailed analysis of John Meier that focuses on the problem of historicity.[1] For the subheadings, I am indebted to Davies and Allison.[2]

The Truth about Jesus

(2) Now when John heard in prison about the deeds of the Christ, he sent word by his disciples, (3) and said to him, "Are you he who is to come, or shall we look for another?" (4) And Jesus answered them, "Go and tell John what you hear and see: the blind see again and the lame walk, lepers are cleansed and the deaf hear, and the dead are raised up, and the poor have good news preached to them. (6) And blessed is he who takes no offense at me." (Matt 11:2-6 = Luke 7:18-23)

The Truth about the Baptist

(7) As they went away, Jesus began to speak to the crowds concerning John, "What did you go out into the wilderness to see? A reed shaken by the wind? (8) Why then did you go out? To see a man clothed in soft raiment? Behold those who wear soft raiment are in kings' houses. (9) Why then did you go out? To see a prophet? Yes, I tell you, and more than a prophet. (10) This is he of whom it is written, 'Behold, I send my messenger before your face, who shall prepare your way before you.' (11) Truly, I say to you among those born of women there has risen no one greater than John the Baptist. Yet he who is least in the kingdom of heaven is greater than he." (Matt 11:7-11 = Luke 7:24-28)

Judgment on Jesus and John

(16) "But to what shall I compare this generation? It is like children sitting in the market places and calling to their playmates, (17) 'We piped to you, and you did not dance. We wailed, and you did not mourn.' (18) For John came neither eating nor drinking, and they say, 'He has a demon.' (19) The Son of Man came eating and drinking, and they say, 'Behold a glutton and a drunkard, a friend of toll-collectors and sinners!' Yet wisdom is justified by her deeds." (Matt 11:16-19 = Luke 7:31-35)

The time frame of the first saying (vv. 2-6) is unambiguous. John has been imprisoned, but obviously has not yet been executed. The fact that he could receive and react to news about what Jesus was doing in Galilee suggests two things. John was being held in Tiberias rather than in Machaerus far to the south and on the other side of the Jordan. And the conditions of his incarceration were not stringent. At this stage apparently John was being held for investigation, as Paul would be in Ephesus some years in the future.[3] Until a decision was made, he was being kept out of circulation.

John's question (v. 3) is meaningless unless Jesus had deviated significantly from the pattern of preaching and practice he had learned from the Baptist. The form of the question does not suggest that Jesus had been negligent. On the contrary, the fact that John thinks of Jesus in terms of the "One Coming" means he was somehow displaying a power John himself felt he did not possess.

John had the humility and common sense to recognize that the impact of his own preaching, even when united to the potent symbol of baptism, would be short-lived. Despite the best will in the world, his converts would inevitably drift back to their old bad habits. Given the imminent danger into which this thrust them (Matt 3:10), John looked forward to the coming of a divine messenger who would be infinitely more effective: "I have baptized you with water; but he will baptize you with the Holy Spirit" (Mark 1:8). John offers no details, presumably because he had no clear idea of whom God would send to complete the task of preparation that John felt was beyond him.[4]

It is extraordinary that John should consider one of his disciples a possible candidate for a role he considered superior to his own. I suspect that, for the first time, he envisaged the possibility that the virgin birth, of which Jesus had told him, might imply the latter was something more than a prophet like Jeremiah (see chapter 4 above).

In his reply Jesus does not reveal his identity. He makes no claim to status. He simply invites John to draw the appropriate conclusion from what Jesus has been saying and doing when viewed against the background of the salvific promises of Isaiah. Let us put together (1) what Jesus said (in bold); (2) the miracles he worked (in italics); and (3) the Isaian texts.

the blind see
Blind man of Bethsaida (Mark 8:22-26)
Bartimaeus (Mark 10:46-54)
Man born blind (John 9:1-7)
"the eyes of the blind shall see" (29:18)
"the eyes of the blind shall be opened" (35:5)

"to open the eyes of the blind" (42:7)
"recovery of sight to the blind" (61:1 LXX)

the lame walk
Paralytic at Capernaum (Mark 2:1-12)
Cripple at Bethesda (John 5:1-9)
"the lame shall leap like a deer" (35:6)

lepers are cleansed
A single leper (Mark 1:40-45)
Ten lepers (Luke 17:11-19)
Lepers are nowhere mentioned in Isaiah.

the deaf hear
Deaf-mute (Mark 7:31-37)
"the deaf shall hear the words" (29:18)
"the ears of the deaf will be unsealed" (35:5)

the dead are raised
Daughter of Jairus (Mark 5:21-43)
Son of the Widow of Nain (Luke 7:11-17)
Lazarus (John 11:1-45)
"Your dead will come back to life" (26:19)

the poor have good news preached to them
The whole preaching ministry of Jesus
"sent to bring good news to the poor" (61:1 LXX)

The only possible conclusion that can be drawn from Jesus' statement is that he believed his words and deeds to be the eschatological blessings Isaiah foretold. His cleansing of lepers, found nowhere in Isaiah, implies that his ministry goes further than Isaiah anticipated.[5] The new age had dawned in his activity, which of course cannot be separated from his person. Therefore, acceptance of Jesus is what makes one blessed (v. 6). No prophet ever made such a claim even implicitly.

Another major difference becomes evident when it is recognized that whereas John stressed the negative, Jesus emphasizes the positive. Their views of divine intervention in history are here diametrically opposed. John spoke of pain and punishment, "every tree therefore that does not bear good fruit is cut down and thrown into the fire" (Matt 3:10). Jesus evokes joy by highlighting healing of the body and nourishment of the spirit by good news. If John's message is "Beware! Repent!" that of Jesus is "Follow me! The kingdom of God is at hand." Manifestly, Jesus has come a long way since he arrived in Galilee where he was first taken to be clone of the Baptist (Mark 6:16).

The authenticity of Matthew 11:2-6 makes it a key witness of Jesus' messianic self-consciousness.[6] Before we come to the key question of how he came to see himself so differently, we must look briefly at the tribute Jesus pays to John the Baptist (Matt 11:7-11). There is general agreement that verses 7-9 were actually spoken by Jesus, but that verse 10 was created subsequently probably to answer the question: in what sense was John the Baptist more than a prophet? Verse 11 is also authentic, but was given its present place here by an editor.[7]

Those who had first known Jesus as a disciple of John must have wondered what he thought of his erstwhile master. Since Jesus was now doing something completely different, would he condemn the Baptist for having been in error? Jesus had no quarrel with what John said. Divine vengeance and retribution are not lacking in the Isaianic prophecies (29:20; 35:4; 61:2) to which Jesus alludes in clarifying his mission, and Jesus never denies divine punishment (Matt 11:21-24). The problem was what John had left unsaid, and Jesus had already dealt with that (vv. 2-6). Here he focuses on the *personality* of John and lavishes praise on his unswerving integrity. He was not deterred by threats or corrupted by wealth and power (vv. 7-11).

The way Jesus does this is extremely clever. Instead of a flat statement and an explicit contrast, he uses rhetorical questions that both compliment John and implicitly criticize the one who had him imprisoned and executed. Antipas had the courtesy title of king, and his early coins carried the symbol of a reed.[8] But since reeds were found in the Jordan where John baptized, and the plural "kings" did not single out an individual, Jesus got his point across without incriminating himself. At one point Antipas considered him a threat, and sought to kill him (Luke 13:31).

Jesus was fully aware of how much he owed John the Baptist. It was in the course of the mission assigned to him by John that he had come to the insight that transformed his understanding of his vocation. Without John, the providential catalyst, that opportunity might never have arisen. Thus he states categorically that John was the greatest person who had ever lived (v. 11a). This has the tone of a panegyric, as if John were already dead. Were this the case it becomes easier to understand why Jesus would take the risk of covertly criticizing Antipas. It also makes better sense of the contrast between John and those who have accepted the rule of God (v. 11b). They are now the most blessed and privileged.[9]

Table Fellowship with Sinners

In the final section (Matt 11:16-19) we move closer to an explanation of Jesus' second conversion, which made his path deviate from that of John. A parable is always polyvalent, but here the children who cry out are Jesus and John. Their different messages were refused, even though logically those who refused one should have accepted the other.

The criticism of John—"he came neither eating or drinking, and you say 'he has a demon'" (v. 18)—cannot be literally true. He would not have lasted a week had he abstained from water. Moreover, we are told that he ate "locusts and wild honey" (Mark 1:6). This was all that was available when he was in the wilderness, but it is a protein-rich diet, and there is no reason to think that he did not accept other food when it was available. Neither the Gospels nor Josephus present John as an ascetic. The fact that John's disciples fasted (Mark 2:18) does not necessarily mean they learned to do so from the Baptist. It is more natural to think of the practice as their response to his execution (Mark 6:29).

More importantly, people might not have responded to John's message through weakness, but there is not the slightest hint they considered him mad. His dress might have been unusual, but the hairy garment had been worn by Elijah (2 Kgs 1:8), one of Israel's greatest prophets. To Jews it would have been a badge of honor rather than evidence of a disturbed mind.[10] According to Josephus, the Baptist was greatly admired: "the crowds were greatly pleased by hearing his words . . . they seemed to do anything that he should advise" (AJ 18.118). In fact, it was due to John's widespread popularity that Antipas had him arrested and executed.

If the criticism of John does not make sense, what is going on here? There is no doubt, as we shall see, that the criticism of Jesus is based on an accurate description of his behavior. It is entirely possible that for increased dramatic effect Jesus created a balancing criticism of John to serve as a foil for the much more severe criticism leveled against himself. If the observation on which the charge against Jesus was based was that he was "eating and drinking," artistry demanded that these activities should be negated for John. But only the deranged abstain from all food and drink. Hence, "he has a demon." The strong element of hyperbole, which is typical of the teaching of Jesus (Matt 3:9; 5:22; 6:3), and his love of antithetic parallelism,[11] tend to confirm the hypothesis of creativity.

What is said of Jesus in Matthew 11:19 falls into three parts:

(a) The Son of Man came eating and drinking;
(b) And they say, "Behold a glutton and a drunkard;
(c) a friend of toll-collectors and sinners."

If we set aside the contrast with John the Baptist, (a) is meaningless, because everyone eats and drinks. It is going much too far to say, as Meier does, that "Jesus the bon vivant . . . offered an easy, joyous way into the kingdom of God."[12] The point of (b) becomes apparent only when (a) and (c) are linked. Jesus was criticized because he ate and drank with toll-collectors and sinners. The reaction (b) is not a dismissive, disparaging remark. According to Deuteronomy, it is a specific legal charge carrying the most serious consequences:

> (18) If someone has a stubborn and rebellious son who will not obey his father and mother, who does not heed them when they discipline him, (19) then his father and his mother shall take hold of him and bring him out to the elders of his town at the gate of that place. (20) They shall say to the elders of his town, "This son of ours is stubborn and rebellious. He will not obey us. He is a glutton and a drunkard." (21) Then all the men of the town shall stone him to death. So you shall purge the evil from your midst; and all Israel will hear, and be afraid. (Deut 21:18-21)

By proclaiming Jesus "a glutton and a drunkard" his accusers are really saying "He is a rebellious son, who is worthy of death." Why should Jesus' eating with toll-collectors and sinners be considered disobedience? What was the nature of his offense?

An invitation to a meal was a gesture of acceptance. It originated in trust and offered protection. In 562 B.C.E. Jehoiachin, king of Judah, was publicly rehabilitated by being brought from prison to the table of Evil-Merodach, king of Babylon (2 Kgs 25:27-30). The hospitality Jesus gave to toll-collectors and sinners inevitably would have been interpreted in the light of such parables as the Great Supper (Matt 22:1-10), the Guest without a Wedding Garment (Matt 22:11-14), and the Ten Virgins (Matt 25:1-13). In these, a banquet symbolized the kingdom of God, and it would have been natural for outsiders to understand Jesus' choice of table companions as a statement that they would inherit the kingdom of God. It was equivalent to a promise that toll-collectors and sinners would be members of the coming kingdom.

Those who made the above inference would have been confirmed in their interpretation by other words of Jesus.

> (27) Depart from me, all you workers of iniquity! (28) There you will weep and gnash your teeth, when you see Abraham and Isaac and Jacob and all the prophets in the kingdom of God and you yourselves thrust out. (29) And men will come from east and west, and from north and south, and sit at table in the kingdom of God. (30) And behold, some are last who will be first, and some are first who will be last. (Luke 13:27-30)

Here presence at a meal is the basis of a stark contrast between believing and unbelieving Jews. "The 'sons of the kingdom' will come to a tragic end because of their response to Jesus and his preaching, while others, less privileged because they have not lived in the land or heard Jesus will find eschatological salvation. The privileged will have their places taken by the underprivileged."[13] And those considered sinners will take the place of those who believed themselves to be righteous at the messianic banquet.

Who Are Sinners?

While the unpopularity of "toll-collectors" is understandable, the stress on sinners demands explanation, because everyone was (and is) in some sense a sinner. Like most, if not all, religions Judaism made a distinction between ordinary sinners and the "lawless," even though the same word ("sinner") was often used for both. Ben Sira exhorts the former, "Have you sinned, my child, do so no more, but pray about your former sins" (21:1), whereas he says of the latter, "The assembly of the lawless (*anomoi*) is like tow gathered together, and their end is a flame of fire. The way of sinners (*hamartoloi*) is smoothly paved with stones, but at its end is the pit of Hades" (21:9-10). Here the parallelism shows that sinner can bear the specialized meaning lawless.

The difference between sinners and lawless was not necessarily the act committed but the attitude behind it. Sinners respected the Law while transgressing it through weakness, while the lawless showed they despised the Law by consciously and consistently refusing to obey at least one specific commandment. For example, the Law forbade the lending of money at interest (Lev 25:36-38), which meant that any Jewish moneylender had chosen an occupation that by definition violated the Law. The only possible inference was that the usurer had no intention of obeying

God. He fell under the condemnation of Ben Sira, "Woe to you, the ungodly, who have forsaken the Law of the Most High God" (41:8).

Even though there would be a gain in clarity by employing lawless to underline the contrast with ordinary sinners, I will use 'sinners' in single quotation marks to mean the lawless in order to make unambiguous the relationship between this background and the situation of Jesus described in the Gospels.

While any Jew might conceivably harbor profound contempt for the Law in his heart while being ostentatiously obedient, this was known to him alone. There were others, however, whose profession was considered to proclaim contempt for the Law and thus to identify the practitioner as a sinner. These were the disreputable occupations of which a representative list is given in the *Mishnah*: "Abba Gorion of Sidon said in the name of Abba Saul: A man should not teach his son to be an ass-driver, or a camel-driver, or a sailor, or a carter, or a herdsman, or a shopkeeper, for their craft is the craft of robbers" (*m. Kiddushin* 4:14; trans. Danby, corrected by Jeremias[14]). These trades were despised because they facilitated dishonesty. They combined temptation and lack of supervision.[15] The first four worked in the transport business. Anyone commissioned to bring goods from A to B was out of sight of both sender and recipient for a considerable time, and who could prove that any loss was not due to accident or robbery rather than theft. A village herdsman was entrusted to take a number of sheep and/or goats from various houses out into the fringes of the desert. Distance ensured that the owner would never know if a kid became a succulent supper for the shepherd. Thus there was a flat prohibition, "No one may buy wool or milk or kids from herdsmen, or wood or fruit from those who watch over fruit trees" (*m. Baba Kamma* 10:9).[16] The idea of a "good" shepherd would have caused eyebrows to rise. A shopkeeper was always in sight of his customer, but unless confronted by the rare expert, he could pass off inferior goods as of first quality or give short weight. There was no need to mention toll-collectors in this list. It went without saying that they were lumped with tax-collectors as sinners because they inevitably abused their powers to enrich themselves dishonestly.

Sinners such as these were not beyond the reach of God's mercy, but in order to be worthy of it they as thieves had to add restitution to repentance.

> If he sins, and so becomes answerable, he must restore what he has taken or demanded in excess: the deposit confided to him, the lost

property that he has found, or any object about which he has perjured himself. He will add one-fifth to the principal and pay the whole to the person who held the property rights on the day when he incurred the guilt. (Lev 5:23-24 = 6:4-5; *m. Baba Kamma* 9:5-6; *m. Baba Metzia* 4:9)[17]

There would have been no criticism of Jesus had his association with sinners been perceived as part of a strategy to persuade them to restore their ill-gotten gains. Those who had attempted to win reparation might be irritated if Jesus succeeded where they had failed, but they had no grounds to object to what he was doing. Had they attempted it, they would have been shouted down by those delighted to recover money they never expected to see again.

Criticism of Jesus becomes understandable only if by his table fellowship with them he was understood to declare symbolically that sinners *while remaining sinners* were admitted to salvation. This brilliant insight of Joachim Jeremias[18] has been developed by Ed Sanders:

> The novelty and offence of Jesus' message was that the wicked [= 'sinners'] who heeded him would be included in the kingdom even though they did not repent as it was universally understood—that is, even though they did not make restitution, sacrifice, and turn to obedience to the law. Jesus offered companionship to the wicked of Israel as a sign that God would save them, and he did not make his association dependent on their conversion to the law. . . . If Jesus added to this such statements as that the tax collectors and prostitutes would enter the kingdom before the righteous (Mt 21:31), the offence would be increased.[19]

At precisely this point we see clearly just how far Jesus had moved away from John the Baptist. John said, "God will forgive you, provided that you repent and mend your ways." Jesus could have said, "God forgives you here and now unconditionally, so naturally in return you will repent and mend your ways." But what he in fact said to a toll-collector, the archetypal sinner, was simply, "Follow me!" (Matt 9:9). He made no demand for restitution or purpose of amendment. Matthew/Levi was accepted the moment he responded, and the association was sealed with a shared meal (Matt 9:10-11).

Rejection of the Law

The implications of Jesus' approach to sinners needs to be spelled out unambiguously. He was rejecting the Law. It can be taken completely for granted at the time of Jesus that the Mosaic Law was considered a unity. All parts were equally the word of God, and thus equally binding (Deut 4:8). There was nothing that could justify picking and choosing among God's words.[20] Jesus, in consequence, could not have refused aspects of the Law without appearing to exhibit the most utter contempt for the Law as such.

This necessary inference from Jesus' table fellowship with sinners is confirmed by his response to the potential convert who asked for leave to bury his father. Jesus said, "Follow me, and let the dead bury their dead" (Matt 8:22). Here Jesus consciously and deliberately issues an order to disobey the fourth commandment, "Honour your father and your mother as Yahweh your God has commanded you" (Deut 5:16).[21] As the formulation explicitly underlines, this was a binding divine precept, and respect for the body of a dead parent certainly came under the umbrella of filial piety. There is evidence that the obligation was considered as of the first importance at the time of Jesus. Certain texts of *m. Berakoth* read, "He whose dead lies unburied before him is exempt . . . from all the duties enjoined in the Law" (3:1),[22] i.e., burial takes precedence over all other obligations until it is completed. Those who have tried to water down the implications of this episode by claiming that "Let the dead bury their dead" is a proverb and should not be taken literally have furnished no response to Hengel's demonstration that no such proverb is attested in the Greco-Roman world, and that such a refusal would contradict not only Jewish but pagan piety.[23] Moreover, it should be noted that Jesus did not allegorize the Law or reinterpret it away or make subtle distinctions. He enunciated a simple, flat refusal of the validity of the Law, which was an implicit claim to sovereign authority.

How then are we to explain the introduction to the antitheses of the Sermon on the Mount? Jesus is represented as saying,

> (17) Think not that I have come to abolish the law and the prophets. I have come not to abolish them but to fulfil them. (18) For truly, I say to you, till heaven and earth pass away, not an iota, not a dot, will pass from the law until all this is accomplished. (19) Whoever then relaxes one of the least of these commandments and teaches men so, shall be called least in the kingdom of heaven; but he who does them and teaches them shall be called great in the kingdom of heaven. (20) For I tell you, unless your righteousness exceeds that of the scribes and Pharisees, you will never enter the kingdom of heaven. (Matt 5:17-20; Luke 16:17)

Fully in conformity with this statement of the principle of strict legalism is Jesus' command to the cured leper to present himself to the priest and to make the offering prescribed by Moses (Matt 8:4; Lev 14:1-32).

Some resolve the tension by refusing to admit the authenticity of these and other dominical sayings, but their arguments are unconvincing.[24] Sayings that insist on the obedience to the Law were spoken by Jesus, and find a perfect setting in the period when he ministered as a disciple of John the Baptist. Then, as we have seen (chapter 4), he was a "zealot" in the classical legalistic sense. Subsequently, as I have argued above, he adopted a radically different attitude toward the Law that proved so scandalous to subsequent generations of his disciples that Luke felt obliged to insert the words "Half of my goods I give to the poor, and if I have defrauded anyone of anything, I restore it fourfold" (Luke 19:8) into the story of Zacchaeus.[25] The addition meant that Jesus did not sit down to eat with a sinner (v. 7) but with one who had repented according to strict Jewish standards.

The Problem of Debt

Now we have to confront the crucial question: why did Jesus reject the Law in asking nothing of sinners? What factors brought him to a decision that ran counter to all the indoctrination he had received as a child and that he had internalized and made his own as a prophetic preacher of repentance with John the Baptist? More specifically, under what conditions would Jesus be forced to admit that a sinner was innocent and not guilty as the Law assumed?

The history of land tenure in Palestine in the century or so before the time of Jesus shows an inexorable absorption of small individual freeholdings into large estates. A little reflection on the economics of a peasant farm will make this process intelligible.[26] The owner and his family contribute their labor. In return the land must supply them with

- enough food to permit the family to live and work.
- fodder for livestock.
- seed for the following year's planting.
- funds in cash or kind to permit trade or barter to satisfy needs beyond the family's skills, e.g., the employment of a builder or a blacksmith.
- funds for special celebrations, e.g., births, deaths, and marriages.
- religious and secular taxes.

Just to list these obligations reveals that the freeholder had no margin for error. The slightest increase in any one sector brought serious trouble. Demand tended to increase, while the economic base was fixed or diminishing. Lack of birth control meant an increasing number of mouths to feed. The rainfall in any given year could be inadequate. The yield from a field could be less than expected; famines occurred with some regularity. A violent storm or a plague of locusts could destroy the crop completely. A broken plow meant delay and a significant cash outlay. A donkey used for plowing and transport might get sick and die, and a replacement cost money. A minor epidemic might carry off a number of close relatives whose funerals had to be paid for. Perhaps two daughters needed dowries at the same time. The double taxation system took a minimum of 40 percent of the peasant's produce,[27] but it could take 60–65 percent.[28]

In order to meet a deficit in any sector, the peasant had no choice but to borrow. This meant temporary release, but he in fact incurred not only the added burden of repayment but also that of interest. In default of an exceptional windfall that would enable a peasant to pay off his debts, it was practically inevitable that he would default, and what he gave as surety would be forfeit to his creditor, namely, all or part of his land, or himself or a member of his family. The alienation of land is self-evident, but Jewish law, in order to pay off a debt, permitted a man to sell himself (Lev 25:39-43) or a daughter under the age of twelve (Exod 21:7) into slavery.[29]

Given his skills, the best option open to a freeholder who lost his land in payment for debt was to rent land. That gave him the dignity of managing his own labor, but all the burdens on the land outlined above were now increased by the addition of rent. If the rent was a percentage of produce, the tenant had a cushion that enabled him to survive bad times. But it could be a fixed quantity of money or produce, in which case all the advantage was on the side of the landlord, who suffered in bad years only when the tenant went bankrupt. Once again debt inevitably reared its ugly head. Failure to pay rent meant eviction.

The next step downward was for the peasant to sell his labor, to work for wages on one of the large estates. But suppose the only job available was that of herdsman. A man with a family to feed, and no choices, could not afford the luxury of refusing employment that would result in him being classed a sinner. He was forced into a lifestyle that he would not have chosen.

How would Jesus have judged such an individual? A hint of how this question might have been answered can be gleaned from his parables dealing with the problem of debt. These, of course, are just stories, but they would have had no point unless they were securely anchored in reality.

In the parable of the Wicked Husbandmen (Mark 12:1-12) we are told of an entrepreneur who set up a vineyard purely as a profit-making industry. He turned it over to tenants, and then disappeared until the rent came due. The hearers of the parable were invited to infer from the violent reaction of the tenants that the amount they had to pay was exorbitant. If they were liable to lose everything by defaulting, they took no real risk by assaulting the rent-collector. The desperation of those crushed by debt is delineated with great economy.

The same problem is evoked graphically in the parable of the Ungrateful Servant (Matt 18:23-35) by the sheer size of the debt. The figure of ten thousand talents is literally unbelievable. The yearly tax revenues of the whole of Judea amounted to only six hundred talents (AJ 17.320). No doubt from personal experience the hearers would immediately have understood the figure from the perspective of the debtor. Under no conceivable circumstances could the debt ever be paid off. The response of the creditor, to sell the whole family into slavery, betrays the conviction of debtors that creditors would never be generous, that they would exact the last cent of any debt and always refuse to extend the deadline, no matter what that did to family members who were in no way responsible. The turnaround of the creditor in the story, who forgave the debt, would have evoked wry shakes of the head, "Would that it were so!" The truth as they knew it was in the second part of the story, the merciless response of the ungrateful servant to the one who owed him a much smaller sum of money.

The parable of the Dishonest Steward (Luke 16:1-8) highlights the distance between creditor and debtor, and the consequent coldness and lack of personal interest. The fact that the steward could reduce with impunity the amount of what was owed to his master reveals that the latter had no real idea of the debts of his tenants. Exaction of payment was a routine matter, and made easier by ignorance of the misery and pain of the debtor's destitution.

A striking contrast appears in the parable of the Two Debtors (Luke 7:40-43). Since it is question of a number of cash loans, the creditor here should be understood as a moneylender.[30] In this instance, however, simply because his debtors could not repay, he cancelled the debt. This was not the way moneylenders normally behaved. Their hardheartedness in resisting the most wrenching appeals was proverbial. Presumably their mothers loved them, but no one else did. Nonetheless, here the inexpressible sense of relief at being free of debt, and thus out of danger of prison or slavery, is described as love.

These four parables yield a series of vivid vignettes that reveal the depth and precision of Jesus' knowledge of the social situation of his hearers. The sympathy with which he entered into the sense of helplessness of those under pressure to do the impossible strongly suggests that he would not have found it in his heart to object to any desperate effort to keep body and soul together.

In other words, Jesus would have seen the herdsman as a victim to be pitied, not a sinner to be ostracized. The erstwhile freeholder deserved God's mercy not condemnation. He had no intention of showing contempt for the Law. What he did was not a matter of choice but of necessity. There was no other work available. Thus, in the eyes of Jesus, he had nothing to repent of, and no restitution to make. Had he taken anything that was not his, it was because it was indispensable to his survival and that of his loved ones. Were blame to be assigned, the religious and civil systems that reduced an individual to such a state were much more worthy recipients.

When this insight flashed into Jesus' mind he must have been profoundly shocked. Hitherto he had lived in obedience to the Law, and as a disciple of John he had demanded such obedience of others. Now he was daring to think that the Law was in error by classifying a victim as a sinner. It is most improbable that he accepted this conclusion easily. The Law was the word of God. How could God be wrong?

There must have been desperate soul-searching as Jesus struggled to reconcile what he *knew* to be the truth with what he was *told* to be the truth. Jesus would have been his own strictest critic. It must have seemed incredibly presumptuous to him to imagine that his judgment should prevail against the wisdom of God. Who was he to set himself against a whole people who accepted the Law without criticism? He sought eagerly for reasons to prove himself wrong. He found none. His intelligence and integrity insisted that he accept reality. Many of those condemned by the Law were not guilty. How long this process took we will never know. But one day he publicly proclaimed his conviction by inviting a sinner to share a meal.

God as Father, not Legislator

Prior to his second conversion Jesus had defined his relationship to God in terms of the Law. Now he had to rethink that relationship, and he had to offer an alternative to the Law to those who listened to him.

We have already seen that in place of John's stress on divine punishment, Jesus insisted on the blessings God channeled though his ministry. We have also noted that he considered many of those condemned by the Law to be worthy of God's mercy. It is not surprising, therefore, that he should have redefined his relationship to God by recognizing him, not as legislator, but as father.

In all five independent strata of tradition in the Gospels, Jesus addresses God as "Father." The implications have been exaggerated due to the assumptions that "Father" always translates *abba,* and that the latter should be rendered "daddy" in order to emphasize the intimacy of the relationship.[31] It is not impossible that Jesus used *abba,* but it is always translated by the formal *patêr* "father." Greek does have terms corresponding to "daddy," namely, *papas/pappas, pappias, pappidion, patridion,*[32] but none of these diminutives appear in the NT.

Nonetheless, the fact that Jesus consistently addressed God as "Father" is unique in first-century Palestinian Judaism. The closest parallels are texts such as "O Lord, Father and Master of my life" (Sir 23:1) and "O Lord, Father and God of my life" (Sir 23:4; cf. 51:10), and "It is your providence, O Father, that steers its course" (Wis 14:3), but all these come from outside Palestine, and are unlikely to have influenced Jesus. Moreover, they call God "Father" in relation to the chosen people, not in relation to any particular individual, the sense in which Jesus used the term. In using "Father," therefore, Jesus claimed to be God's son in a unique and intimate way that had eschatological significance (Mark 12:6; Luke 22:29). Moreover, he transmitted that sonship to his followers by teaching them to pray as he did (Luke 11:2).[33]

The Touchstone of Salvation

In thus presenting himself as a model of prayer, Jesus implicitly made himself the touchstone of salvation, a distinction previously enjoyed by the Law. His exemplary activity replaces the Law. Jesus made the same point implicitly by taking over a classic formulation of contemporary Judaism to articulate his own self-understanding.[34] The *Aboth of Rabbi Nathan* said, "The person who hears the *words of the law and does good works* builds on solid ground" (24; cf. Deut 28:1, 15). Jesus, however, said, "Everyone then who hears *these words of mine and does them* will be like a wise man who built his house upon rock" (Matt 7:24). In both texts the emphasis is on "hearing" and "doing," which implies that there may be "hearing" without "doing," but the focus is entirely different. "Words of the Law" are replaced by "these words of mine." A literal translation of the Greek is "of me these words," which gives the personal pronoun dramatic emphasis by placing it first. Jesus is clearly thinking of other "words" while asserting the supreme importance of his own.

But what do "my words" mean? Matthew answers this question by juxtaposing another saying of Jesus, "Not everyone who says to me 'Lord, Lord' shall enter the kingdom of heaven, but he who does the will of my Father who is in heaven" (Matt 7:21). The words of Jesus articulate the will of his Father, as the Law once expressed the will of God. The content, however, remains obscure until we recall that Matthew 7:24 belongs to a parable that is Jesus' last word in the Sermon on the Mount (Matt 5:1–7:27). In compiling this collection of Jesus' sayings Matthew fills out what is meant by "the Good News of the kingdom" (Matt 4:23).

The strongest expression of this line of thought occurs in Q: "So everyone who acknowledges me before men, I also will acknowledge before my Father who is in heaven. But whoever denies me before men, I also will deny before my Father who is in heaven" (Matt 10:32-33). "And I tell you, everyone who acknowledges me before men, the Son of Man also will acknowledge before the angels of God. But he who denies me before men will be denied before the angels of God" (Luke 12:8-9). In contrast to the immediacy of Matthew, where only Jesus and his Father are in view, Luke's version gives prominence to two intermediaries, the Son of Man and the angels of God. Jesus and God do not appear at all. Which version better preserves the words of Jesus?

Some scholars[35] think Luke's version is the original because at the time of Jesus any thought of a final judgment would have evoked the extraordinary scene in Daniel 7:1-28, in which a Son of Man appears. In consequence, they maintain, Jesus would have used language appropriate to Daniel 7. This line of argument, however, ignores major differences between Luke's version and Daniel 7. In the latter, the Son of Man is entirely inactive. In particular, he does not act as advocate or accuser. Angels are not mentioned at all. In other words, what is specific to Luke does not appear in Daniel, and any direct allusion is highly problematic.

More importantly this approach fails to give any weight to the fact that the emphatic use of the first person singular is solidly rooted in the authentic Jesus tradition,[36] e.g., in authoritative pronouncements, "Amen,

I say to you" (Matt 5:18, etc.), and in healing stories, "I command you, come out of him" (Mark 9:25). This is all the more significant in that Matthew never replaces "Son of Man" by "I."[37] It is much more likely, in my view, that Luke disguised the radicalism of the authentic version preserved by Matthew by introducing surrogates for Jesus and God. It was typical of the early church to tone down statements deemed too scandalous for public consumption.[38]

Even if Matthew's version is secondary, it only makes absolutely clear what is implied by Luke. The claim is in fact extraordinary. Jesus has immediate access to God who accepts without question his estimate of the eternal worth of a person. The acceptance or refusal of Jesus is the criterion by which humanity will be judged.

The possibility that there will be those who fail to acknowledge Jesus before men unambiguously indicates Jesus' awareness that his disciples would be challenged.[39] This did not demand any exceptional foresight. If his critics considered Jesus a rebellious son worthy of death (Matt 11:19), was it not inevitable that his followers also would be subject to persecution? The infection had to be eradicated completely from the midst of the Jewish people. Thus, perhaps as the clouds of hostility became ever darker,[40] Jesus warned his disciples that personal testimony to his status and authority would be required of them in situations that might lead to martyrdom. Peter was in fact so challenged in the courtyard of the high priest, and failed the test (Mark 14:66-72).

It is not necessary for my purpose here to go further into Jesus' self-understanding. Enough has been said to show that to speak of his second "conversion" is not to play with words. At some point in his ministry in Galilee, Jesus underwent a radical change in his attitude toward God and the Law that he could not have foreseen when he committed himself to the mission of John the Baptist and that he would certainly have repudiated had the thought entered his mind.

Paul

In opposition to Jesus whose second conversion must be deduced from the contradiction in his behavior patterns, Paul speaks of his second conversion on a number of occasions and in different ways; a greatly exaggerated list is given by Seyoon Kim.[41]

An appropriate place to begin is with his confession of a change in his appreciation of Jesus Christ. "From now on, therefore, we know no one in a fleshly way. Even though we once knew Christ in a fleshly way, we know him so no longer" (2 Cor 5:16). In this translation "in a fleshly way" translates *kata sarka*. This Greek phrase, however, is used by Paul both as an adverb and as an adjective. In the past the adjectival sense was given priority because then the second part of the verse would read "we once knew Christ according to the flesh," i.e., "in the flesh," which could be interpreted as meaning that Paul had encountered Christ during his earthly ministry. This, of course, opened the door to all sorts of speculation. One scholar went so far as to postulate that Paul was the rich young man who lacked the courage to accept the invitation of Jesus (Mark 10:17-20)!

Closer attention to Pauline usage, however, has revealed that the structure of a phrase using *kata sarka* is different in the two usages. When used as an adjective *kata sarka* always follows the noun it qualifies (Rom 9:3; 1 Cor 1:26; 10:18). Here, however, it precedes "Christ," and thus must be understood as an adverb modifying the verb "to know," which in fact is the predominant usage in Paul.[42] This conclusion is confirmed by the first part of the verse where *kata sarka* simply cannot be understood adjectivally, because the sentence would then mean that Paul knew nobody personally.[43]

Paul is speaking of a true and false way of assessing Christ that should then translate into a true and false way of estimating other human beings. He now has abandoned the false way in which he once knew Christ. When contrasted with the authentic way of knowing displayed in Paul's total commitment to Christ as the one who has inaugurated the New Age, this repudiated knowledge can only refer to the way Paul the Pharisee thought of Christ.

At that stage of his life Paul accepted, as a minimum, the common estimation of his colleagues, which is reflected no doubt rather accurately in a passage from Josephus that originally read:[44]

> Now there was about this time Jesus, a wise man. He was a doer of unbelievable deeds, and a teacher of those with an appetite for novelties. He drew over to him both many of the Jews and of the Gentiles. And when Pilate, at the suggestion of the principal men among us, had condemned him to the cross, those that loved him at first did not forsake him. And the tribe of Messianists so named from him are not extinct at this day (AJ 18.63-64).

Here Josephus damns Jesus with faint praise. The underlying assessment is that Jesus was a charlatan who preyed on the credulous. Given Paul's persecution of Jesus' followers, it is likely that his judgment would have been much harsher. He would have dismissed Jesus as deranged, so preposterous was his claim to sit in judgment on the Law, and probably as evil, insofar as he consciously and deliberately led other Jews astray, thereby putting them at risk of eternal punishment.

Encounter with the Risen Lord

What happened to change Paul's mind? The simplest answer he gives is that "he saw Jesus our Lord" (1 Cor 9:1). What exactly he meant by this needs clarification that Paul provides some chapters later. After mentioning the death and resurrection of Christ, he continues:

> (5) He appeared to Cephas, then to the twelve. (6) Then he appeared to more than 500 brethren at one time, most of whom are still alive, though some have fallen asleep. (7) Then he appeared to James, then to all the apostles. (8) Last of all, as to one untimely born, he appeared also to me, (9) for I am the least of the apostles, unfit to be called an apostle, because I persecuted the church of God. (1 Cor 15:6-9)

Paul here ranks his conversion with the experience of others who had encountered the risen Lord in a way that changed their lives. A number of these stories are given in the Gospels. We hear of appearances to a single person, Mary Magdalen or Thomas, to a couple on their way to Emmaus, and to a group of the disciples. All these recognition appearances exhibit the same fourfold pattern:

(1) **The death of Jesus is the end**.

Mary weeps at the tomb (John 20:11). Cleopas confesses deep disappointment (Luke 24:21). Disciples hide in fear (John 20:19). Thomas mocks (John 20:25).

(2) **Jesus intervenes**.

He calls Mary (John 20:16). He joins Cleopas (Luke 24:15). He appears in the midst of the disciples (John 20:19). Jesus came (John 20:26).

(3) **Jesus offers a sign of his identity**.

He shows his hands and side (John 20:20). He shows his hands and feet (Luke 24:40). He breaks bread (Luke 24:30). He offers his hands and side (John 20:27).

(4) **Jesus is recognized.**

They worshiped him (Matt 28:9). Mary says "Rabboni" (John 20:16). Their eyes were opened and they recognized him (Luke 24:31). They saw the Lord (John 20:20). "My Lord and my God!" (John 20:28).

Stage 1 is certainly justified in the case of Paul. There is no doubt he believed that the death of Jesus was the end of his mischief-making. He was totally concerned with the correction of Jesus' disciples and their return to the observance of the Law as the sole prerequisite for salvation. Jesus was no longer on the scene and could not intervene. He could be dismissed without qualm. We can be sure, in consequence, that Paul did not expect anything to happen as he trudged toward Damascus. In this he was one with those who had followed Jesus during his lifetime, but who had not really believed his promise that he would rise from the dead.

Stage 4 is equally verified in Paul's case. Whatever the nature of the experience he emerged with the absolute conviction that the Jesus of Nazareth, who had been crucified under Pontius Pilate, was alive. Paul could not have been unaware that Jesus was believed to have risen from the dead. Not only was it a topic that greatly interested Pharisees,[45] but it was the basis of the conviction of Jesus' disciples that he was the Messiah. Resurrection put the divine stamp of approval on everything Jesus had said and done. It must have been on the lips of his disciples every time they spoke. It was the unique experience integral to the story on which their new identity was based.

Now Paul had to confront the implications of the fact that the belief of those whom he had persecuted was literally true. It was not a metaphorical way of speaking of the survival of Jesus' soul after death. Pharisees did not believe in that sort of dualistic anthropology in which body and soul were not only distinguishable but separable. They held for the traditional Jewish monistic anthropology in which the person had to be spoken of as "an animated body" or "an embodied soul," or any formula that made it clear that there was no soul without a body or vice versa. As far as Paul was concerned, there was only one way to be alive, and Jesus existed in precisely that way.

Stages 2 and 3 in the four-part recognition appearance pattern remain mysteries as far as Paul is concerned. He does not tell us in what form Jesus appeared, and we are ignorant of how Paul recognized someone that he had never seen in his life before. The questions implied in both these statements manifestly also occurred to Luke because he answers them.

Luke gives three accounts of Paul's conversion that differ in details (Acts 9:3-19; 22:6-16; 26:12-18). A glance at a synopsis,[46] however, reveals that the core of the experience is identical in all three narratives. Paul sees only a bright light from heaven. A voice addresses him by name, "Saul, Saul, why do you persecute me?" In response Paul inquires regarding the identity of the speaker, "Who are you Lord?" and gets the answer "I am Jesus [the Nazarene] whom you are persecuting."

The scene could hardly be set with greater precision. The protagonists are formally identified, and the objectivity of the event is attested by witnesses. Here, there is some variety among the accounts in what was seen and heard, but two out of the three agree Paul was led blind to Damascus, where, by the intervention of Ananias, he was cured. The miracle guaranteed the divine origin of the experience. Like other converts Paul was then baptized and received the Holy Spirit.

Luke, in other words, answers all the questions that one might have regarding Paul's conversion after reading the sparse allusions that the apostle himself makes to the most important experience of his life. Only the fact mattered to Paul, not the modality. He gravely underestimated the interest of believers in how precisely he changed from a persecutor to a follower of Jesus. The turnaround was so drastic that an explanation was necessary. Luke saw that by satisfying this curiosity he could print an indelible portrait of Paul on the minds of his readers. Luke was also perhaps aware that some believers did not fully trust this new Paul (cf. Gal 1:23), saying in effect, "He claims to have had an encounter with Jesus, but has he submitted to baptism, and thus publicly committed himself as a believer?" In dealing with these problems there is no reason to think Luke had privileged information as to what actually happened. Some have suggested that he drew on material in Galatians and 2 Corinthians, but if so, this in no way diminishes the extent to which Luke drew on his imagination. It was in a good cause, and things might well have happened that way.

Lord, Christ, and Son of God

One of the things Paul tells us about his conversion explains how it defined his relationship with Jesus. "I was apprehended by Christ Jesus" (Phil 3:12). It is difficult to find an adequate translation for the Greek verb used here, *katalambanō,* but given Paul's attitude toward Christ and Christians at that moment, the connotation must be "to seize with hostile intent" (BAGD 413, 1b). The underlying idea is well brought out by Bruce: "Paul recalls his conversion as the occasion on which a powerful hand was laid on his shoulder, turning him right around in his tracks, and a voice that brooked no refusal spoke in his ear, 'You must come along with me.'"[47] Similarly Kim: "[Jesus] arrested him with overwhelming power."[48]

It would be difficult, if not impossible, to find a more graphic illustration of an act of lordship. Hence, Paul's first conviction regarding the true identity of Jesus of Nazareth was that he was "Lord." Subsequently Paul makes clear his feeling that he was "compelled" to preach the Gospel (1 Cor 9:16). He also claimed to live under pressure that confined and restricted him (2 Cor 5:14).

Once Paul had experienced Jesus as "Lord" he had to acknowledge him as "Christ." Jesus was not just any Lord but the Jewish Messiah for whom Paul hoped, and who had been the basis of his persecution of the followers of Jesus. Moreover, if Jesus was the Messiah, he was also "the Son of God" in a unique way because these two concepts were inseparable in Judaism.[49]

Thus right from the very beginning of his life as a Christian "Jesus," "Christ," "Lord," and "Son of God" were intimately associated in Paul's mind. They were rooted in his experience as interpreted in the light of his Pharisaic background. There was no need for him to learn them from the churches in Damascus or Jerusalem. Rather, he felt at home in such communities because their confession of Jesus as Lord revealed to him that their experience of the Risen One was identical with his. Their proclamation resonated in his heart. Their words articulated his feelings about Jesus.

Paul's recognition that his conversion was a moment of illumination can also be expressed very differently. "(11) I would have you know that the gospel which I preached is not according to man. (12) For I did not receive it from man, nor was I taught it, but (it came) through a revelation of Jesus Christ" (Gal 1:11-12). Here Paul both accepts and refuses. He denies the source of his Gospel was human, and that instruction was the means whereby he acquired his Gospel. He affirms that he received its content through revelation.

If taken at face value, this would seem to suggest that all the ideas contained in Paul's preaching were flashed into his mind from on high in the moment of his encounter with Christ. This extreme interpretation does violence to common sense. These two verses articulate the thesis that Paul will demonstrate in Galatians 1–2.[50] It flatly contradicts the criticism of his opponents that he falsified the message he was commissioned to preach, and that the Galatians in consequence should reject what they had learned from him. Given Paul's violent temperament, an element of hyperbole crept into the formulation of his thesis (contrast the more sober 1 Cor 15:1-3), but there is also a solid foundation of truth in what he says.

Paul's mind was not a blank when he encountered Jesus. We have seen Paul's confession that he had rejected false knowledge of Jesus (2 Cor 5:16). What that means is that his assessment of certain claims made by Jesus or his disciples has altered. Whereas he once dismissed as preposterous the claims that Jesus was the Messiah, who had been raised from the dead, now he knew those claims to be absolute truth, and they were the essence of his Gospel. These were not new ideas, however, but old ones seen from a different perspective. Moreover, they were not concepts he had learned in the way that he had imbibed his knowledge of the Law from teachers. They were simply part of the information he had picked up about Jesus and his movement. To see familiar things from a radically new angle can legitimately be described as a revelation. The trigger of this insight was his encounter with the risen Lord.

When examined closely, therefore, it is clear that there is a sense in which Galatians 1:11-12 is literally true. It is equally obvious, however, that the formulation is virtually an invitation to misunderstanding. It could easily be understood to assert a much greater claim, namely, to superhuman knowledge. This ability to combine the defensible and the untenable in a single sentence testifies to Paul's literary genius. His back was against the wall, and he was quite happy to throw dust in the eyes of his enemies.

In reality, of course, following his conversion Paul did go on to learn much more about the historical Jesus from those who had been his companions.[51] It is extremely improbable that he spent his two weeks with Peter talking about fishing or the health of the latter's mother-in-law (Gal 1:18).

Rejection of the Law

Like Jesus, Paul's second conversion also meant rejection of the Law. The two decisions, however, were very different. For Jesus it must have been a slow, wrenching, traumatic choice to go against everything in which he had hitherto believed, particularly since he had no guarantee he was right. Paul, on the contrary, was mentally well prepared for the switch, and he experienced no ambivalence.

All the groundwork had been done during Paul's persecution of Christians (see chapter 4). Their presence in Jerusalem had forced him to think through the Law/Messiah problem. He disagreed violently with their "both-and" approach, and concluded that it was an "either-or" issue. It had to be one or the other. If the Law was still in vigor, the Messiah could not have come. Equally, if the Messiah had in fact arrived, then there was no further place for the Law. The moment Paul accepted Jesus as the Messiah, his mental preparation was such that his commitment to the Law ceased without a twinge of regret. The Law had had its day; it was no longer relevant. Jesus the risen Lord and Christ had chosen him. This was Paul's guarantee. It gave him the certitude that he was right in abandoning the Law.

In a gesture as dramatic as Jesus' repudiation of the fourth commandment (Matt 8:22), Paul confirmed his rejection of the Law by going to Arabia (Gal 1:17). "Arabia" then is roughly the eastern part of the kingdom of Jordan today. It was settled by the Nabataeans whose capital was Petra. Paul's choice fixed on that area because it was virtually guaranteed he would find no Jews there.[52] The Nabataean Aretas IV had gone to war with Antipas of Galilee because of the latter's repudiation of his daughter. In response to his defeat, Antipas delated Aretas to the emperor Tiberius, whose tolerance of wars between client kings on the eastern frontier was minimal. The Nabataeans waited in fear and trembling for the Roman axe to descend. As months lengthened into years, Nabataean anxiety was transmuted into bitter anger at the Jews who had created the intolerable situation. No Jew would have been welcome in Nabataean territory, and Jewish traders in Damascus must have suffered from the loss of a lucrative market.

It is most unlikely that Paul got far into Arabia or spent much time there. The mission was inspired by his zeal, not his intelligence. The significance of the gesture is that it demonstrates he immediately drew the most important conclusion from the irrelevance of the Law. The criteria for salvation it laid down were now meaningless. Gentiles, in consequence, had access to salvation simply by following Christ.

For perhaps fifteen years after his conversion Paul tolerated the observance of the Law in his communities. As far as he was concerned, it had absolutely no significance in terms of salvation, but if Jewish converts to Christianity wished to circumcise their children and to eat only kosher food, they were welcome to continue to observe their ancestral customs. Their salvation, however, depended exclusively on faith in Jesus Christ.

This attitude permitted Antioch-on-the-Orontes to flourish as a mixed community. Believers from both Judaism and paganism lived amicably together, and were even able to share meals that witnessed publicly to the unity of the community. This delicate balancing act was brutally disrupted by the arrival of agents from the conservative wing of the church in Jerusalem, who insisted on raising the standard of observance to the point where Jewish believers could no longer eat with Gentile converts unless the latter effectively became Jews by adopting the same standard of kashrut (Gal 2:11-14).

The conclusion that Paul drew from this incident was that his tolerance had been a mistake. Thereafter he became radically antinomian. His new position was stated with great precision by James some years later in order to alert Paul to the danger he ran from Jerusalemites zealous for the Law: "They have been told about you that you teach all the Jews who are among the Gentiles to forsake Moses, telling them not to circumcise their children or observe the customs" (Acts 21:21). Hitherto Paul had seen the Law as just another factor, and not an important one, in the human matrix. Antioch forced him to realize that to give the Law any place, however minor, in a Christian community was to create a rival to Christ. Once the Law was admitted to a community, legalism was also invited in. It was much easier to debate points of law than to discern the needs of one's neighbor. Only parts of oneself were involved in observing a list of commandments. One had to be totally dedicated to model one's life on the Christ "who loved me and gave himself for me" (Gal 2:20). Paul had come a long way from his days as a Pharisee when he said "The whole Law is fulfilled in one word, 'You shall love your neighbor as yourself'" (Gal 5:14) and "Bear one another's burdens and so fulfill the law which is Christ" (Gal 6:2).

Finances

Great battles were fought in the hearts and minds of Jesus and Paul as they struggled to realize their destiny, but they did not live in a spiritual vacuum. They had to eat, drink, and sleep. Who paid? In terms of financing, the coincidences between Paul and Jesus are complex. There are similarities, but also related differences.

No matter how minimalist his lifestyle in Judea and Galilee, Jesus must have had some means of support. There is no hint that he continued to practice the trade that presumably he had learned from Joseph. The Gospels give the impression that he had no time to earn a living. Perhaps he was supported at least in part by his family when he worked in partnership with John. Once Jesus had rejected the Law, however, it is unlikely they continued. The meager evidence we have shows hostility, not sympathy. His mother and siblings, considering him mad, were ashamed of the show that he was making of himself, and tried to get him away from the crowds (Mark 3:20-35). His brothers thought he should save the family embarrassment by preaching in Judea (John 7:3) where they were unknown. It would appear, therefore, that to continue his mission in Galilee and Jerusalem, Jesus had to rely on the charity of converts (Luke 8:3; John 12:6), and availed of the hospitality of Peter in Capernaum (Mark 1:29; 2:1) when he was in Galilee (Matt 8:20) and of Martha, Mary, and Lazarus in Bethany (John 11:5) when he was in the Jerusalem area.

As we have seen, Paul was educated in a way that implied he did not have to work. Unlike Jesus, therefore, he had not learned a trade as a young man. But he did so in later life. At the point where Jesus abandoned his trade because his ministry was so absorbing, Paul became a tentmaker in order to give himself missionary mobility by acquiring a skill in demand throughout the whole of the eastern Mediterranean.[53]

During his temporary vocation Paul, like Jesus, presumably enjoyed family support in addition to institutionalized Jerusalem charity. At that stage of their careers both brought honor to their families and would have been subsidized with pride. Once Paul rejected the Law, however, it is likely the subsidies stopped. It would be a way of bringing him to his senses. The revenues from his trade (1 Thess 2:9; 2 Thess 3:7-9; 1 Cor 4:12) sufficed until the number of converts in any given city reached a critical mass. Then, like Jesus, he had to rely on the charity of converts (Phil 4:16; 2 Cor 11:8).

Notes

[1] John P. Meier, *A Marginal Jew. Rethinking the Historical Jesus. II. Mentor, Message and Miracles* (New York: Doubleday, 1994) 2:130–233.

[2] W. D. Davies and Dale Allison, *A Critical and Exegetical Commentary on the Gospel of Matthew. II. Chs. 8–18,* International Critical Commentary (Edinburgh: Clark, 1991) 259.

[3] Jerome Murphy-O'Connor, *Paul. A Critical Life* (Oxford: Clarendon Press, 1996) 175–79.

[4] Meier, *A Marginal Jew. Rethinking the Historical Jesus. II. Mentor, Message and Miracles,* 35.

[5] Davies and Allison, *A Critical and Exegetical Commentary on the Gospel of Matthew*. II. *Chs. 8–18*, 243.

[6] Ibid., 245.

[7] Ibid., 246.

[8] Meier, *A Marginal Jew. Rethinking the Historical Jesus*. II. *Mentor, Message and Miracles*, 139.

[9] Davies and Allison, *A Critical and Exegetical Commentary on the Gospel of Matthew*. II. *Chs. 8–18*, 254.

[10] As against ibid., 263.

[11] Joachim Jeremias, *New Testament Theology*. I. *The Proclamation of Jesus* (London: SCM Press, 1971) 19.

[12] Meier, *A Marginal Jew. Rethinking the Historical Jesus*. II. *Mentor, Message and Miracles*, 149.

[13] Davies and Allison, *A Critical and Exegetical Commentary on the Gospel of Matthew*. II. *Chs. 8–18*, 28.

[14] Joachim Jeremias, *Jerusalem in the Time of Jesus. An Investigation into Economic and Social Conditions during the New Testament Period* (London: SCM Press, 1969) 304.

[15] Ibid., 305.

[16] Danby, *The Mishnah*, 347.

[17] Ibid., 344, 354.

[18] Jeremias, *New Testament Theology*. I. *The Proclamation of Jesus*, 177.

[19] E. P. Sanders, *Jesus and Judaism* (Philadelphia: Fortress, 1985) 207–8.

[20] Ibid., 247.

[21] Ibid., 252–55.

[22] See Herbert Danby, *The Mishnah* (Oxford: Oxford University Press, 1933).

[23] Martin Hengl, *The Charismatic Leader and His Followers* (Edinburgh: Clark, 1981) 8–15.

[24] For example, Sanders, *Jesus and Judaism*, 261–63.

[25] Joseph A. Fitzmyer, *The Gospel according to Luke (X–XXIV)* (New York: Doubleday, 1985) 1221.

[26] Douglas E. Oakman, *Jesus and the Economic Questions of His Day*, Studies in the Bible and Early Christianity 8 (Lewiston, NY: Mellen Press, 1986) 49–57.

[27] Sean Freyne, *Galilee, Jesus and the Gospels. Literary Approaches and Historical Investigations* (Dublin: Gill and Macmillan, 1988) 164.

[28] Oakman, *Jesus and the Economic Questions of His Day*, 72.

[29] Jeremias, *Jerusalem in the Time of Jesus*, 313.

[30] Joseph A. Fitzmyer, *The Gospel according to Luke (I–IX)* (New York: Doubleday, 1981) 690.

[31] See Jeremias, *New Testament Theology*. I. *The Proclamation of Jesus*, 61–68.

[32] James Barr, "Abba Isn't 'Daddy,'" *Journal of Theological Studies* 39 (1988) 38.

[33] James D. G. Dunn, *Christology in the Making. An Inquiry into the Origins of the Doctrine of the Incarnation* (London: SCM Press, 1980) 28.

[34] Jeremias, *New Testament Theology. I. The Proclamation of Jesus,* 254.

[35] For example, Davies and Allison, *A Critical and Exegetical Commentary on the Gospel of Matthew.* II. *Chs. 8–18,* 214.

[36] Jeremias, *New Testament Theology. I. The Proclamation of Jesus,* 250–53.

[37] Norman Perrin, *Rediscovering the Teaching of Jesus* (New York: Harper & Row, 1976) 189.

[38] Ibid., 39.

[39] Davies and Allison, *A Critical and Exegetical Commentary on the Gospel of Matthew.* II. *Chs. 8–18,* 215.

[40] Ulrich Luz, *Das Evangelium nach Matthäus.* 2 Teilband. Mt 8–17. Evangelish-katholischer Kommentar zum Neuen Testament 1/2 (Zurich: Benziger/Neukirchen: Neukirchener Verlag, 1990) 124.

[41] Seyoon Kim, *The Origin of Paul's Gospel,* 2nd edition (Tübingen: Mohr Siebeck, 1984) 3–31.

[42] J. Louis Martyn, *Theological Issues in the Letters of Paul* (Edinburgh: Clark, 1997a) 91.

[43] C. K. Barrett, *A Commentary on the Second Epistle to the Corinthians,* Harper's NT Commentaries (New York: Harper, 1973) 171.

[44] Murphy-O'Connor, *Paul. A Critical Life,* 74–75.

[45] Harry Sysling, *Tehiyyat Ha-Metim. The Resurrection of the Dead in the Palestinian Targums of the Pentateuch and the Parallel Traditions in Classical Rabbinic Literature,* Texte und Studien zum Antiken Judentum 57 (Tübingen: Mohr Siebeck, 1996).

[46] For example, David Stanley, "Paul's Conversion in Acts: Why the Three Accounts?" *Catholic Biblical Quarterly* 15 (1953) 323–24; or Charles Hedrick, "Paul's Conversion/Call: A Comparative Analysis of the Three Reports in Acts," *Journal of Biblical Literature* 100 (1981) 417–18.

[47] F. F. Bruce, *Philippians,* New International Bible Commentary (Peabody, MA: Hendrickson, 1989) 200.

[48] Kim, *The Origin of Paul's Gospel,* 108.

[49] John Collins, *The Scepter and the Star. The Messiahs of the Dead Sea Scrolls and Other Ancient Literature,* Anchor Bible Reference Library (New York: Doubleday, 1995) 169.

[50] Louis J. Martyn, "Galatians," in *The Anchor Bible* (New York: Doubleday, 1997b) 136.

[51] James D. G. Dunn, *The Theology of Paul the Apostle* (Grand Rapids, MI: Eerdmans, 1998) 182–95.

[52] Jerome Murphy-O'Connor, "Paul in Arabia," *Catholic Biblical Quarterly* 55 (1993) 732–37.

[53] Jerome Murphy-O'Connor, "Prisca and Aquila. Travelling Tent-Makers and Church-Builders," *Bible Review* 8/6 (1992) 40–51.

Chapter 6

Execution by the Romans

*T*he *final parallel between the lives of Jesus and Paul is that both were executed by the Roman authorities. Jesus died under Pontius Pilate on Friday 7 April 30 C.E. in Jerusalem. Paul expired in Rome under the emperor Nero in the autumn of 67 C.E. Jesus just happened to be in the wrong place at the wrong time. Paul went looking for trouble. Although the same authority was responsible, Paul's clean death by decapitation contrasted brutally with the long, drawn-out agony of Jesus.*

Jesus

Each of the four Gospels contains an account of the passion of Jesus. A quick study of the following table will reveal three salient points.

Event	Matthew	Mark	Luke	John
Gethsemani	26:36-46	14:32-42	22:39-46	18:1
Arrest	26:47-56	14:43-52	22:47-53	18:2-12
High Priest	26:57-68	14:53-65	22:54-71	18:13-24
To Pilate	27:1-2	15:1	23:1	18:28
Judas' Death	27:3-10			
Pilate	27:11-14	15:2-5	23:2-5	18:29-38
Herod			23:6-12	
Innocent			23:13-16	
Choice	27:15-23	15:6-14	23:17-23	18:39-40
Sentence	27:24-26	15:15	23:24-25	19:1, 16
Mockery	27:27-31a	15:16-20a		19:2-3

Via Dolorosa	27:31b-32	15:20b-21	23:26-32	19:17a
Crucifixion	27:33-37	15:22-26	23:33-34	19:17b-27
Derided	27:38-43	15:27-32a	23:35-38	
Two Thieves	27:44	15:32b	23:39-43	19:18
Death	27:45-54	15:33-39	23:44-48	19:28-30
Witnesses	27:55-56	15:40-41	23:49	19:25-27
Side Pierced				19:31-37
Burial	27:57-61	15:42-47	23:50-56	19:38-42

First, all four gospels preserve precisely the same order of events. Compare the list in the left-hand column with the chapters and verses in the other columns.

Second, there are differences. The most important are signaled by gaps in the columns. The death of Judas appears solely in Matthew. Only in Luke is Jesus sent to Herod Antipas. The innocence of Jesus is a major issue only in Luke, who alone does not have the scene of the mockery of Jesus by the soldiers. The soldiers' piercing the side of Jesus is exclusive to John.

Third, the similarities and the differences are not of the same quality. The differences are peripheral in the sense that they do not affect the core of the narrative that is to be found in the similarities.

This particular combination of identity in essentials and divergence in marginals points to one certain conclusion. We are dealing with a foundational narrative that not only began in oral tradition, but that continued to conserve its salient features.

Laws of Oral Tradition

Every group needs a story to found its identity. Separation from others has to be justified. The first Christians were no exception. They had separated from other Jews and so had to justify their adherence to the Jesus movement. The way they did this was by telling stories about him. In revealing what attracted them to him they also explained who he was and what he did. Very quickly individual stories were absorbed into the group story. Particular elements were sacrificed to clearly delineated essentials. Once this basic story was established, consistency in its retelling was essential to the unity of the group. In consequence, its retelling was tightly controlled. The early Christians knew, however, that each retelling was a unique performance the storyteller tailored to the audience.

A certain flexibility had to be permitted if the story was to retain its freshness and vitality. In other words, the audience was prepared to accept and appreciate variety and creativity in ancillary details provided that the invariable core story reinforced the group's self-understanding. The storyteller operated within clear parameters understood by everyone. The hearers were not there to be informed (the story was already familiar) but to be confirmed in their identity.

In simplified form these are what have been observed to be the most important laws of oral tradition.[1] Their relevance to our study of the passion narrative becomes clear if we substitute "evangelist" for "storyteller." Since the four evangelists spoke to different audiences, we should expect their accounts to vary, not only in peripheral details of what they have in common, but in the presence or absence of whole episodes. Such variations cannot be dealt with here. The question of what is likely to have happened can be addressed only to the common denominators, i.e., those elements that appear in three or four versions of the same episode.

At Gethsemani

The very first episode highlights the necessity of bringing a critical judgment even to accounts where the evangelists have a great deal in common. Clearly, Jesus had a traumatic experience in the Garden at Gethsemani. But when he moved away from the disciples to pray alone, their weary eyes closed in sleep (Mark 14:37). How then did they know what words he said? Clearly, they could have had no idea. We are forced to conclude that the evangelists subsequently put into the mouth of Jesus the sentiments they imagined they would feel if they knew they were facing the possibility of torture and death. The eyewitnesses fully appreciated the shuddering horror integral to the intense emotional state of Jesus (Mark 14:33) and wanted no follower of Jesus to be under any misapprehension. Gethsemani inaugurated a process that came to a terrible end.

The arrest of Jesus was ordered by the chief priests (Mark 14:43), who played a prime role in the passion of Jesus.[2] No one in this shadowy group is ever named, but in Jewish sources they appear as a distinct body within the sacerdotal hierarchy of the Temple that functioned as an executive committee.[3] Since membership carried great power, it is assumed that sons of the most eminent and privileged priestly families had certain advantages in promotion.

Why should the Jewish authorities have acted against Jesus at just this particular moment? The majority of scholars would agree with Dunn "that if there was any single incident which triggered the move to arrest Jesus it was his 'prophetic sign' in the Temple."[4] This is the occasion when Jesus overturned the tables of the moneychangers, an event the Synoptics present as occurring in the last weeks of Jesus' life (Mark 11:15-17). No doubt this is what the three evangelists intended to suggest; it is never formally asserted. Their motive was to provide a basis for the accusation of the high priest (see below). Such a late date for "the cleansing of the Temple," however, is most improbable. The interpretation given above (chapter 4) confirms John's placing of this event at the very beginning of the ministry of Jesus (2:13-17). Moreover, a failed attempt to disrupt Temple worship, which lasted no longer than ten or fifteen minutes, was not likely to inflame the mob. Hence, it does not explain why it was so urgent to act against Jesus immediately despite the proximity of Passover.

Regarding the Fourth Gospel, we do not have to rely on an uncertain inference. The causal link is stated unambiguously. "From that day [the raising of Lazarus] they took counsel how to put him to death" (John 11:53; cf. 12:10). It is not necessary to establish that the miracle really occurred.[5] The mere rumor of such an event would have been sufficient to raise to fever pitch whatever apprehensions the chief priests had regarding Jesus. He had to be removed as quickly as possible before he became a rallying point for the pilgrims pouring into the city. Thus Jesus was arrested as soon as he emerged from hiding (John 11:54).

In the House of the High Priest

The actual arrest would have been carried out by the Levites who, as a quasi-police force, kept order in the Temple.[6] They brought Jesus to the high priest, Caiaphas. According to Matthew, Mark, and Luke, he convened the whole Sanhedrin, thereby inviting the Gospel readers to envisage a formal judicial process. Were this in fact the case, we should expect the trial to have taken place in "the Hall beside the Xystus" on the west side of the Temple Mount where the Sanhedrin normally assembled.[7] All four evangelists, however, tell us that the meeting took place in the *house* of the high priest.[8] Luke alone makes this explicit (22:54), but immediately goes on to mention the internal courtyard (*aulê*)—a standard feature in any large house—the other evangelists identify as "the courtyard of the high priest" (Mark 14:54; Matt 26:58;

John 18:15). The high priest probably lived in the area of fine houses known as Mount Sion today.

The location forces us to think not of a public trial, but rather of a private meeting to which the high priest summoned a number of senior advisors, some no doubt drawn from the chief priests. These were "the principal men among us" mentioned by Josephus (AJ 18.63-64). The exaggeration of the number of those present (the whole Sanhedrin) is standard storytelling hyperbole. The time is another indication that there was no formal trial. The Sanhedrin could not initiate a prosecution at night (*m. Sanhedrin* 4.1).

No disciples of Jesus were present at that conclave. How then did they know who was there or what was said? The curiosity of Jesus' followers cannot be gainsaid, and it would have taken little to loosen the tongues of attendants or guards. The names of the participants would have been of little interest. Everyone knew they were officials with power. The charge was another matter, because it might touch the disciples of Jesus directly. They had fled from Gethsemani (Mark 14:50) and might need to go further afield.

Even though it is reported only by Mark and Matthew that Jesus was accused of promising to destroy the Temple and build it again, this double charge is given a high degree of historical probability.[9] Jesus is recalled as having preached the destruction of the Temple in Mark (13:2), Q (Matt 23:38), Luke (Acts 6:14), and the Gospel of Thomas (71). In John's version of the cleansing of the Temple, Jesus says, "Destroy this temple and in three days I will raise it up" (2:19).

Such wide attestation is confirmed by the fact that both elements of the charge would have been of particular *personal* importance to the high priest and the chief priests. The Temple was the source of their political power and material wealth. Without a temple they would lose everything. For a sacerdotal caste, a place of sacrifice was essential, and for Jews there could be no temple outside Jerusalem. The truth of this is demonstrated by the disappearance of high priest and chief priests when the Romans destroyed the Temple in 70. All that remains are the names Cohen and Levi.

Ever since the grave damage done to the Temple by the Babylonians and the Seleucids, its continuing existence was always a matter of great political sensitivity. Any threat against it was guaranteed to be taken seriously, and it was elementary common sense to take measures to ensure it could not possibly happen. Even though Jesus may only have spoken of the destruction of the Temple in general terms (e.g., Mark 13:2) as part of his pessimistic vision of the future of Jerusalem (Mark 13:3-37), it was in the interest of both his partisans and his opponents to transform a prediction into a threat. For the former it exalted Jesus' power, whereas for the latter it apparently made the problem easier to deal with.

Jesus did not respond to the charge. The high priest then asked him, "Are you the Christ, the Son of the Blessed?" (Mark 14:61). At first sight there appears to be no connection with what has gone before. Dunn, however, has shown that the question emerges from the *second* part of the charge, namely, that Jesus promised to rebuild the Temple.[10] One of the Dead Sea Scrolls (4Q174 1.10-13) demonstrates that in the first century the prophecy of Nathan to David regarding his son Solomon was understood to refer to a royal Messiah:

> (12) When your days are fulfilled and you lie down with your ancestors, I will raise up your offspring after you, who shall come forth from your body, and I will establish his kingdom. (13) He shall build a house for my name, and I will establish the throne of his kingdom forever. (14) I will be a father to him, and he shall be a son to me. (2 Sam 7:12-14; cf. Zech 6:12-13)

The prophecy looks forward (1) to a son of David (v. 12), (2) who would build the Temple (v. 13), and (3) whom God would regard as his Son (v. 14). As Dunn puts it very effectively, Caiaphas asked Jesus, "You are charged with promising to build the Temple. Do you then claim to fulfil Nathan's prophecy? Are you the royal Messiah, God's son?"[11] The high priest's tone, of course, would have been one of extreme incredulity. Mark portrays Jesus as answering with a flat affirmative "I am" (14:62), but in this he stands alone. The ambiguity of the response provided by the other evangelists is probably closer to historical truth.[12]

The high priest interpreted Jesus' refusal to deny the charge as blasphemy, which carried the death penalty (Lev 24:15-16), but he could go no further. He and his advisors wanted Jesus dead. Whatever the rights or wrongs of the present situation, his removal would put an end to any future problems. The Jews, however, had no authority to execute anyone (John 18:31). The Romans reserved that privilege to themselves. In turbulent Palestine the last thing they would have done was to give any group of Jews the means to remove pro-Roman factions.[13] Even the autocratic Herod the Great did not dare execute his sons who plotted to remove him without Roman authorization (JW 1.537, 661).

The high priest, therefore, had to transform a religious charge into a political one. This was not difficult. Once the label of royal Messiah had been attached to Jesus in the minds of the Jewish authorities, it was but a short and easy step to say Jesus was claiming to be king of the Jews.[14] This shift would be all the easier if someone remembered that Jesus preached a coming kingdom that was already breaking into the present in his actions.[15] This was the main theme of his ministry, and cannot have been unknown. A new kingdom, however, was by definition opposed to the existing political order that was determined by Rome. To proclaim the kingdom of God was treason. The stage was now set for the transfer of Jesus from Jewish jurisdiction to that of Pontius Pilate.

In the Praetorium of Pilate

Pilate was ensconced in the palace built by Herod the Great in the northwest corner of first-century Jerusalem. In Aramaic it was known as Gabbatha, which identifies it as the highest point in the city (John 19:13). It served as the residence of the Roman procurators when they came up from Caesarea to ensure there were no disturbances that might have political overtones during the great feasts that drew great numbers of pilgrims to Jerusalem. Philo calls the palace "the house of the procurators" (*Legatio ad Gaium*, 306).

The hints of the Gospels that Pilate's judgment chair was set on an open-air platform projected out from the east side of the palace is confirmed by Josephus: "Florus [one of Pilate's successors] took up his quarters at the palace, and on the next day he had his tribunal set before it, and sat upon it" (JW 2.301).

Precisely because so little is known about Pilate, legends have grown up around him.[16] The one salient fact all other judgments must take into account is that he was Prefect of Judea for at least eleven years, from 26 to 37 C.E.[17] To have survived for so long he must have been extremely shrewd and capable of recovering quickly from any mistakes. Even though the emperor forced him to back down twice when the Jews laid charges against him, he was evidently too valuable to be removed. There can be no doubt, however, that both sides cordially detested each other, and that there was a strong element of friction in all their relationships. The extent to which this fact dominates Pilate's dealing with Jesus is not always recognized.

Understandably Pilate begins with the accusation, "Are you the king of the Jews?" Jesus, once again, refuses to say yes or no. Pilate then proclaims the innocence of Jesus. If the Jews really wanted a victim, he offered Barabbas as an alternative. This attitude has caused some scholars to accuse the evangelists of whitewashing Pilate by making him appear pro-Christian, thereby shifting the blame for Jesus' death to the Jews. Nothing could be further from the truth.

It would be extremely naive to imagine that Pilate relied on the Jewish authorities for information about Jesus. He certainly had his own efficient intelligence service, and was as fully informed as the high priest regarding any threat to public order in Judea and Samaria. It is perfectly possible, therefore, that he was aware of Jesus' activity and did not consider him a security danger because he had no significant following. When seen from this perspective, Pilate's reaction to the accusation against Jesus is perfectly in character. It is most unlikely that he had any strong feelings about Jesus one way or the other. But he realized that he was being manipulated, and deeply resented the insult. He knew perfectly well that to pronounce Jesus innocent would embarrass the Jewish authorities by forcing them to insist on arguments they would have great difficulty in proving. To play with them was pleasant revenge.

While delighting in seeing the chief priests squirm, Pilate was fully aware they would have no hesitation in delating him to Rome if he gave them the slightest excuse. Should there be something in their accusation, and he did not act on the information, then his career would be at risk.

Truth and justice were not factors in Pilate's judgment. He might have been under certain theoretical restraints regarding Roman citizens, but in reality a provincial governor was not restricted in any way as to what he could consider a crime or accept as evidence. Only Pilate's superior in far-off Antioch-on-the-Orontes had the authority to question his decisions, and one would have to be extremely well connected to get his ear. Like any other official in his position, Pilate would have neither qualm nor scruple about solving a difficulty or preventing a potential future problem by means of an arbitrary execution. According to Josephus, the execution of John the Baptist was simply a precaution. Antipas decided that "it would be much better to strike first and be rid of him before his activity led to an uprising" (AJ 18.118).

Having decided that his self-interest would be best served by accepting the accusation of the Jewish authorities, Pilate condemned Jesus to death (Mark 15:15). His choice of crucifixion may have been just a whim. His colleague Flaccus, the Prefect of Egypt, had Jews tortured and crucified in the amphitheater of Alexandria merely to entertain the crowd (Philo, *Flaccus*, 83–4). In both cases it also served to remind all Jews of who was in charge.

The scourging of one condemned to death might appear rather gratuitous, but it was in fact a standard part of the punishment. We are told concerning one of Pilate's successors in Jerusalem in 66 C.E., "Florus ventured then to do what no one had done before, that is, to have men of the equestrian order scourged and nailed to the cross before his tribunal, who although they were Jews by birth had the dignity of Romans" (JW 2.308). Roman death sentences were always carried out by soldiers. Thus a duty centurion supervised the scourging of Jesus and commanded the execution party that led Jesus through the city. The prisoner had the crossbeam strapped to his shoulders and outspread arms (Plutarch, *Moralia* 554B).

The Route to Golgotha

At one point the centurion compelled Simon of Cyrene, who just happened to be passing, to assist Jesus (Mark 15:20b). This was most unusual. It would appear that the scourging had been too enthusiastic, and that Jesus had lost a lot of blood. It would go hard with the centurion if Jesus died before reaching the place of execution. Under such circumstances, to dragoon a bystander to help carry the cross was a sensible precaution. It was more important that Jesus should be alive when he was crucified than that he should carry the crossbeam the whole way. The historicity of this incident is guaranteed by the fact that no evangelist would invent Jesus' failure to carry his cross.

Movement through Jerusalem would have been unusually difficult that particular Friday. It was the eve of Passover, and around fifteen thousand lambs had to be sacrificed to meet the needs of the population swollen by pilgrims. The streets were crowded with men dragging frantic lambs to the Temple, and others carrying home the carcasses for the Passover meal in the evening. A small execution party escorting three criminals would have generated resentment rather than excitement. They would have been seen as another obstacle in an already frustrating day. It is most improbable, therefore, that "there followed him a great multitude of the people and of women who bewailed and lamented him" (Luke 23:27).

There was no fixed execution place in Jerusalem. Death sentences were usually passed and carried out in Caesarea. Thus the centurion had to find a site, and his choice fell on an abandoned quarry just outside the Gennath Gate in the north wall. A large mass of poor softish stone projected into the quarry from the east side. It had eroded in such a way as to give the impression of a skull, perhaps holes resembling eyes. Hence the Hebrew name Golgotha (John 19:17).

No limits were put on the sadism of the executioners. The victim could be attached to the cross either with nails or with cords (Pliny, *Natural History* 28.46). Since they inflicted much greater pain, nails were far more common, and would be assumed in the case of Jesus, even if we did not have the words of Thomas that he would not believe, "unless I see in his hands the print of the nails and put my finger in the mark of the nails" (John 20:25).

The victim hung in excruciating pain. In addition to the abrasion of nerves by the nails, he had to try to raise himself to breathe by pushing on his nailed feet. If he drooped he experienced the agony of suffocation. The presence of the women in the vicinity of the cross of Jesus protected him from crows perching on his shoulder to pick out his eyes, and wild dogs leaping up to pull off flesh from any part they could reach.

Jesus was fortunate to have lost so much blood in the scourging that he only endured three hours on the cross, from noon to 3:00 P.M. (Mark 15:33). If the Gospel accounts are combined, Jesus spoke seven times. It was virtually impossible, however, for a crucified man to say anything. He barely had enough breath to groan. Moreover, each saying is recorded by only one evangelist. It is more probable, therefore, that they put what they felt to be appropriate words in the mouth of Jesus.[18]

It was normal Roman practice for victims to be left hanging for as long as it took to die. Jewish law, however, specified that the bodies of the crucified should be removed from the cross before sunset (Deut 21:22-23). This gave the chief priests another opportunity to bend Pilate to their will. They insisted that the Law be applied. His instinct would have been to refuse, but he was shrewd enough to realize that such a gratuitous insult to the Law might provoke a riot. Thus he sent soldiers to Golgotha. They had orders to kill the three victims before dumping the bodies at the foot of the crosses. Disposal was a matter for the Jews. Jesus looked as if he were already dead, so they applied the standard test of pricking him with the point of a weapon. The two thieves were still alive, so they ensured they died quickly by breaking their legs (John 19:31-34). This meant they could no longer raise themselves to breathe, and suffocated.

On the opposite side of the quarry, an entrepreneur had taken advantage of the vertical rock face to create a walk-in catacomb. There, because it was close; and because the time was short, they laid the body of Jesus in the outermost chamber (John 19:41-42).

Paul

Paul had many brushes with Roman authorities throughout his career. The Roman provinces of Syria, Cilicia, Galatia, Asia, Macedonia, and Achaia were his mission field. In virtually every province he got into trouble. In city after city he caused what he modestly calls a "tumult" (2 Cor 6:5). In the Acts of the Apostles, Luke provides a list:

Galatia	Pisidian Antioch (13:50)
	Iconium (14:5-6)
	Lystra (14:19)
Asia	Ephesus (19:23-41)
Macedonia	Philippi (16:22)
	Thessalonica (17:5-9)
	Beroea (17:13)
Achaia	Corinth (18:12-17)

Understandably, any conscientious official would hold him for investigation. With an undertone of pride Paul tells us he was imprisoned on many occasions (2 Cor 6:5; 11:23). Only two, however, are documented: in Philippi (Acts 16:24-40), and in Ephesus (deduced from Philippians and Philemon).

We pick up Paul's story, however, on his last visit to Jerusalem. In the early summer of 56 C.E. he brought to Jerusalem the money for the poor he had promised on his previous visit in the autumn of 51 C.E. This gift from his communities in Europe and Asia Minor was intended to narrow the widening gap between Gentile and Jewish wings of the church. Nonetheless Paul was desperately worried about the reception he would get (Rom 15:31). As soon as he arrived, James, the head of the church in Jerusalem, made it clear to him that he had every reason to be seriously concerned (Acts 21:21). His reputation among Jews was very bad. Not only had he himself abandoned his ancestral faith, but he attempted to persuade others to do likewise.

Not surprisingly, when this charge was made in public (Acts 21:28) a riot developed, and Paul was in real danger of being lynched. An alert Roman sentry high on the tower of the Antonia fortress called out the guard. The tribune arrested him for his own good (Acts 21:33) and, when it appeared there might be an assassination attempt on Paul, sent him off to one of Pilate's successors, the governor Felix in Caesarea (Acts 23:26).

Up to this point the Romans had saved Paul's life twice. Neither Felix nor his successor Festus were in any hurry to do anything about Paul. After some two years of frustration he eventually exercised his right as a Roman citizen to be judged by the emperor (Acts 25:11). After many adventures, Paul made it to Rome, where Luke's narrative ends without telling us anything about Paul's fate.

Many scholars believe nothing more can be said. These, however, reject the three Pastoral Epistles. Their methodology leaves much to be desired insofar as it assumes for 2 Timothy what can be proved for 1 Timothy and Titus. The two latter letters are certainly inauthentic, but if 2 Timothy is examined in and for itself, nothing in it militates against its having been written by Paul.[19] From its contents we can infer a perfectly plausible account of Paul's last years.

It is clear from 2 Timothy that Paul was liberated. Despite the opposition of the Roman church, which knew he had no chance of success, he insisted on making his planned visit to Spain (Rom 15:24). It proved to be just as much a mistake as his mission to Arabia (Gal 1:17). With his tail between his legs he returned to the east. The only place where Paul had unfinished business was in Illyricum (Rom 15:19). He had been forced to abort his ministry there in the summer of 55 c.e. because of the need to resolve serious problems at Corinth. He could not have stayed there more than a year or so without stunting the natural development of the community. Then he had to move on.

Somewhat wistfully no doubt, but with the feeling that he was not really wanted or needed, Paul wandered east along the Via Egnatia visiting his thriving foundations in Thessalonica and Philippi in Macedonia before crossing over to Troas in Asia. His mood was further depressed when he arrived in Ephesus. It quickly emerged that Timothy, who had been a wonderful assistant, was not an effective leader (2 Tim 1:6, 8; 2:3, 15). Paul had to find an excuse to move him out and take over himself. Paul quickly realized, however, that he did not have the support of the community; "all who are in Asia have turned away from me" (2 Tim 1:15). With great humility he moved to Miletus (2 Tim 4:20), which was far enough away that he would not be an irritant, but close enough should the Ephesians have need of him. There for the first time in several years he ministered in virgin territory. He was an apostle once again.

The Persecution of Nero

This fruitful and absorbing ministry came to an abrupt end in the late summer of 65 C.E. The report of the frightful tortures Nero was inflicting on Christians in Rome flashed across the Roman world. The rumor that he had started the fire that destroyed ten of the fourteen regions of Rome in June 64 C.E. was becoming dangerous. He had to find another something to interest the mob.

> To suppress this rumour, Nero fabricated scapegoats, and punished with every refinement the notoriously depraved Christians (as they were popularly called) . . . Their deaths were made farcical. Dressed in wild animals' skins, they were torn to pieces by dogs, or crucified, or made into torches to be ignited after dark as substitutes for daylight. Nero provided his Gardens for the spectacle, and exhibited displays in the Circus, at which he mingled with the crowd, or stood in a chariot, dressed as a charioteer. (Tacitus, *Annals* 15.44; trans. Grant)[20]

No doubt Paul and his converts had accepted the idea of martyrdom as a remote future possibility. Now they had to face reality. The effect of a vision of an extremely painful, prolonged death was disastrous. Seeing the impact of Nero's bestial ferocity on those around him, Paul's sympathetic imagination vividly recreated the profound shock of those Christians in Rome who had escaped the imperial dragnet. He could smell the fear that the frightfulness on the Palatine and in the Circus had generated.

It was obvious to Paul that the church in Rome had been shaken to its foundations. There was real danger of disintegration. Aid from outside was imperative to restore morale. Words would have been of little use. Roman believers needed to see other Christians putting their lives on the line by coming to stand with them. This was not something Paul could ask of others. But he himself? No one depended on him. His life expectancy was not great. And he had wondered if he was really needed anymore. Did he recall what he had once written? "The love of Christ constrains us, because we are convinced that one has died for all; therefore all have died. And he died that those who live might live no longer for themselves, but for him who for their sake died and was raised" (2 Cor 5:14-15).

It is entirely possible that when Paul went to Rome for the second and last time he thought of a death like that of Jesus. But he was not planning to die. He was not looking for martyrdom. There was still much work to be done, as we shall see below, and this was the decisive factor. He had already confronted the dilemma of death versus life when the Roman governor had him imprisoned at Ephesus, and reasoned out his response.

> (20) With full courage now as always Christ will be honored in my body, whether by life or by death. (21) For to me to live is Christ and to die is gain. (22) If it is to be life in the flesh, that means fruitful labor for me. Yet which I shall choose I cannot tell. (23) I am hard pressed between the two. My desire is to depart and be with Christ, for that is far better, (24) But to remain in the flesh is more necessary on your account. (Phil 1:20-24)

Clearly for Paul what was best in theory (union with Christ), and personally desirable (an easier life), was not the basis for a moral judgment (v. 23). The love shown by Christ was his criterion (2 Cor 5:14). This meant that the needs of others were paramount in any moral choice (v. 24; cf. 1 Cor 8:11). If there was a whole empire to be converted, Paul did not believe he had the right to opt for heavenly comfort.

But, if death was God's decision, then Paul would accept it. For a long time he had faced up to the fact that he might die for his faith. He had written to the Corinthians that he "always carried in the body the dying of Jesus" in the sense that "while we live we are always being given up to death for Jesus" (2 Cor 4:10-11). Every hour he felt he was in peril; imaginatively he died every day (1 Cor 15:30-31). He was mentally prepared to confront the terrors of Nero's Rome.

Once he had made up his mind, Paul moved quickly, even though it meant abandoning a sick companion (2 Tim 4:20). Possibly it was nearing the end of the sailing season, and he feared being stuck in Miletus for the winter. It must have been immensely gratifying for Paul that he did not have to travel alone. His little entourage unanimously opted to go with him. Trophimus, however, could not be moved, and Tychicus was needed in Ephesus (2 Tim 4:12). Erastus had second thoughts as they sailed west and, as they crossed the isthmus on foot, he left the group in his hometown, Corinth (2 Tim 4:20; Rom 16:23).

Paul was able to relax only when they were safely across the Adriatic Sea. They still had 340 miles on the Via Appia to cover, but they were safe from the winter sailing closure. By the time they arrived in Rome in the autumn of 65 c.e. the worst of the persecution was over. It had served its purpose and the citizens of Rome already had something else to occupy their attention. In 65 c.e. a group of those who had lost valuable land in the great fire of Rome plotted to assassinate Nero and put

Gaius Calpurnius Piso on the throne. The conspiracy was revealed, and the resulting executions gave the Romans plenty to talk about. Thereafter Nero suspected everyone, and heads rolled at a whim.

Now, however, they were the heads of the upper class. The emperor's anger did not reach down into the proletariat. Not only were they no threat, but they admired him for his generosity and the lavish entertainments he provided. It was to this section of the population that the great majority of Christians belonged. The shadow of danger had lifted, and Paul believed that believers should return to their vigorous apostolate. An infusion of fearlessness was the antidote for terror-driven apathy.

Imprisoned in Rome

This was not entirely to the liking of the Christians in Rome. The last thing they wanted was to have the imperial spotlight shine in their direction once again. They knew the fickleness of Nero. Paul, in their eyes, was an outsider and a troublemaker. They were the ones who had suffered. It was their responsibility to determine their own road to recovery. His arrogant assumption of leadership carried the wounding implication that they were skulking cowards.

Just how deeply the Roman believers resented Paul became evident when he was eventually arrested. On the occasion of his first appearance before the magistrate, absolutely no one turned up to support him by their presence and prayers. He wrote bitterly, "all abandoned me" (2 Tim 4:16). Did he think of the disciples of Jesus who fled from Gethsemani (Mark 14:40), leaving him alone as he had predicted (John 16:32)?

The purpose of this preliminary examination was to determine the identity of the accused and the general validity of the charges against him. It was held in public, and supporters were permitted to testify, to encourage, and even to advise on points of law.[21] If reputable citizens spoke out forcibly in favor of the accused, he had a very good chance of being discharged, particularly if it appeared the accusation had been motivated by malice.

The fact that Paul had no relations, friends, or even business contacts to identify him naturally made the magistrate very suspicious. As a self-confessed Christian (2 Tim 4:17), was Paul perhaps in Rome to take revenge on the emperor for his treatment of other members of his movement? Might he have connections with those members of the nobility who desired nothing more than to get rid of Nero, and who might provide logistical support for a fanatical assassin with his own agenda?

These possibilities alone would make any prudent magistrate pronounce a verdict of *Amplius* "More." Further information was required. To ensure that the defendant did not slip away into the anonymity of the Roman underworld, he had to be held until his situation was clarified. Moreover, a magistrate who knew the way the wind was blowing in Rome would have deferred any action until after consultation with the political echelon. As in the case of Jesus, truth and justice did not weigh in the balance against bureaucratic survival.

Paul, in consequence, was held "in chains" as a "hardened criminal" (2 Tim 2:9). The Christians of Rome ignored him. His one visitor was Onesiphorus, who had come all the way from Ephesus to give him support (2 Tim 1:16-17). But then something happened that cost him his life (2 Tim 1:18). Perhaps an accident, or more likely a senseless murder for a few coppers in a backstreet of Rome. Paul must have been shattered.

Paul's sense of isolation increased as those who had come with him from the east drifted away (2 Tim 4:9-11). This suggests that his incarceration had dragged on longer than anyone had expected—probably all of 66 C.E. and into the early part of the following year. Demas had run to Thessalonica in search of security. The same note of disgust does not appear when Paul mentions the departure of Crescens and Titus. Presumably they went to mission fields in Gaul/Galatia and Dalmatia respectively. The fact that Paul does not speak warmly of their initiative hints that the self-absorption he showed during a previous imprisonment (Phil 1:17-18) still lay just beneath the surface. Luke, he informs Timothy pathetically, is the only one to remain with him. The community on which he depended was reduced to just one other person.

A Letter from Prison

If Paul wrote more than one letter from his Roman prison, they have not survived. The one preserved (2 Tim) is not quite what might have been expected from one in his precarious position. It is not a last will and testament. Nor does it discuss weighty matters of life and death, or glorify martyrdom. Despite Paul's depression and loneliness, it is a surprisingly upbeat piece of practical planning. It must have been written in the spring of 67 C.E. if the anticipated events were to take place during the period when travel was possible (April–September).

Timothy was somewhere in Asia because on his way to Rome he had to pick up the cloak, scrolls, and notebooks Paul had left behind in Troas (2 Tim 4:13). It would take the letter at least two months to cover the twelve hundred miles that separated Paul and Timothy, and a further two months for Timothy to reach Rome.

Here we see the optimistic side of Paul's character. Despite his present circumstances he fully expected to be alive in four or five months from the writing of the letter and, in addition, to be free to work in cooperation with Timothy and Mark. This, after all, was the wisdom of experience. In the past all his examinations by Roman authorities had ended in his being set free. He could not imagine what new evidence might be produced at his second hearing.

Yet this time, at the back of his mind, Paul was not entirely sure. His imprisonment had gone on much longer than usual. Something was not quite right. A clear sense of finality is manifest in the most explicitly self-revelatory words that Paul ever wrote.

> As for me, I am already being poured out as a libation, and the time of my departure has come. I have fought the good fight, I have finished the race. I have kept the faith. From now on there is reserved for me the crown of righteousness, which the Lord, the righteous judge, will give me on that day, and not only to me but also to all who have longed for his appearing. (2 Tim 4:6-8)

The sense of completion could not be more emphatic, and the words have been understood as Paul's recognition that his execution date had been set. But this cannot be correct. We saw above that he fully expected to be alive in five months' time. These words rather reflect the complacent awareness of a life well spent.

Paul, who by now was over seventy, realized his best years were behind him. He had given his all in the arena or battleground of life. In terms of the normal lifespan, he was living on borrowed time, particularly for one who for so many years had borne in his body the dying of Jesus (2 Cor 4:10). Each day was a grace, and he intended to make the best possible use of every moment. He might not live long after his release from prison, but that did not exempt him from the obligations of his ministry. He could plan for the future and, if he was taken, then Timothy and Mark could carry on.

Sentence of Death

Paul's optimism was misplaced. In the last quarter of 67 c.e. he was again summoned before the magistrate. This time the decision went against him. The mere fact that he admitted to being a Christian was sufficient (2 Tim 4:17). Nero had established the sinister precedent that the guilt of Christians could be presumed, and that the appropriate penalty was death.

Roman law offered a choice to one condemned to death (OCD 580). Originally the magistrate was obliged to give the condemned the opportunity to escape after the sentence had been passed. Under Tiberius (14–37 c.e.) such voluntary permanent exile was replaced by a formal sentence of deportation to a particular place, normally an island such as Gyara, combined with loss of citizenship and property. Were Paul in fact confronted with this choice, he would certainly have chosen exile. As we saw above, life for him was fruitful labor (Phil 1:21-25). He was an *apostle* with an obligation from which no one could release him to proclaim the gospel. Gyara might not be the ideal place to live, but there were souls there to be saved, and he would meet many others on the long journey to the east.

If we accept the witness of Eusebius—"It is recorded that in Nero's reign Paul was beheaded in Rome" (*History of the Church* 2.25; cf. 3.1)[22]— we must conclude Paul was not given the choice that was his right. The magistrate no doubt felt it prudent to follow the example of the emperor in considering it imperative to execute any Christian brought before him. He did not demean himself, however, by ordering the sort of torture that had made Nero a monster of depravity. Paul, as befitted a Roman citizen, should be beheaded. The death of a Galilean peasant was much more drawn out and cruel.

It is unlikely that Paul had to wait long for the sentence to be carried out. In any case, he needed little time to prepare his soul. The usual convulsion of the instinct of self-preservation would have been brought under control quickly. For one who had striven throughout his ministry "to manifest in the body the life of Jesus" (2 Cor 4:10-11), it was the supreme grace to have the opportunity to die in witness as Jesus had done. Paul's "desire to depart and to be with Christ" (Phil 1:23) was finally realized under the best possible conditions. As he serenely bared his neck for the sword of the executioner, he knew his death would be the resonant proclamation that he had kept the faith.

Notes

[1] James D. G. Dunn, *Christianity in the Making*. I. *Jesus Remembered* (Grand Rapids, MI: Eerdmans, 2003) 192–210.

[2] E. P. Sanders, *Jesus and Judaism* (Philadelphia: Fortress, 1985) 310–11.

[3] Joachim Jeremias, *Jerusalem in the Time of Jesus. An Investigation into Economic and Social Conditions during the New Testament Period* (London: SCM Press, 1969) 179.

[4] Dunn, *Christianity in the Making*. I. *Jesus Remembered*, 769.

[5] John P. Meier, *A Marginal Jew. Rethinking the Historical Jesus*. II. *Mentor, Message and Miracles* (New York: Doubleday, 1994) 831.

[6] Jeremias, *Jerusalem in the Time of Jesus. An Investigation into Economic and Social Conditions during the New Testament Period*, 209–10.

[7] Emil Schürer, *The History of the Jewish People in the Age of Jesus Christ (175 BC–AD 135)* (Edinburgh: Clark, 1973) 2:224.

[8] Raymond E. Brown, *The Death of the Messiah. From Gethsemane to the Grave*, Anchor Bible Reference Library (New York: Doubleday, 1994) 403.

[9] Dunn, *Christianity in the Making*. I. *Jesus Remembered*, 632.

[10] Ibid., 633.

[11] Ibid.

[12] Ibid., 652.

[13] A. N. Sherwin-White, *Roman Society and Roman Law in the New Testament* (Oxford: Clarendon Press, 1963) 36–37.

[14] Dunn, *Christianity in the Making*. I. *Jesus Remembered*, 634.

[15] Meier, *A Marginal Jew. Rethinking the Historical Jesus*. II. *Mentor, Message and Miracles*, 450–54.

[16] Ann Wroe, *Pontius Pilate. The Biography of an Invented Man* (New York: Random House, 2000).

[17] Daniel R. Schwartz, "Pontius Pilate" in *Anchor Bible Dictionary* (New York: Doubleday. 1992) 5:395–401.

[18] Dunn, *Christianity in the Making*. I. *Jesus Remembered*, 780.

[19] Jerome Murphy-O'Connor, *Paul. A Critical Life* (Oxford: Clarendon Press, 1996) 356–59.

[20] M. Grant, *Tacitus. The Annals of Imperial Rome* (London: Penquin Books, 1996) 365.

[21] Ceslas Spicq, *Les Épitres Pastorales*, Études Bibliques (Paris: Gabalda, 1969) 818.

[22] G. A. Williamson, *Eusebius. The History of the Church from Christ to Constantine* (London: Penguin Books, 1989) 62.

Conclusion

Greatly exaggerated conclusions have been drawn from coincidences. Most recently, in his *Jesus Was Caesar: On the Julian Origin of Christianity* (2004), Francesco Carotta maintains, on the basis of what he sees as a series of parallels—for example, Jesus and Caesar have the same initials, one crossed the Rubicon while the other crossed the Jordan, etc.—that the Gospels are no more than a second-century C.E. rewriting of the story of Julius Caesar. For a reason that is never explained, someone thought it worthwhile to invent a figure called Jesus Christ, and to give him a life modeled on that of Julius Caesar. Any explanation of why there should be four versions of the career of Jesus is also carefully avoided.

To emphasize the parallels between Jesus and Paul might appear to suggest that I believe Paul arranged the crucial moments of his life to coincide with those in the life of Jesus. Nothing could be further from the truth. There is no doubt that Paul thought of himself as another Christ. He told the Corinthians,

> We always carry in the body the dying of Jesus so that the life of Jesus may be manifested in our bodies. While we live we are always being given up to death on account of Jesus, so that the life of Jesus may be manifested in our mortal flesh. (2 Cor 4:10-11)

Here Paul claims to incarnate the humanity of Jesus. Clearly, however, this refers to his moral comportment and missionary dedication. He is so committed to Jesus as his role model that he mirrors the Jesus that he invites others to follow: "Imitate me, as I imitate Christ" (1 Cor 11:1). The resemblance to Christ is rooted, not in any superficial similarity in the successive events of their lives, but in his success in "putting on Christ" (Gal 3:27).

The first three parallels—birth, refugee, alien environment—are events over which Paul had absolutely no control. They cannot possibly have been planned acts of imitation. Regarding Paul's temporary vocation, he had made the decision to become a Pharisee at least ten years *before* Jesus opted to partner John the Baptist. The time factor excludes imitation. Paul's second conversion certainly involved the intention to model his life on that of Jesus. To this end he consciously accumulated information regarding the words and deeds of the historical Jesus (Gal 1:18). It is not impossible, therefore, that Paul hoped his death would come at the hands of the Romans, but there is not the slightest hint he manipulated circumstances to bring this about.

The parallels in themselves do not tell us anything new about Jesus or Paul. Their value is to focus attention on critical moments or aspects of their lives that are not given the importance they deserve in more wide-ranging studies. The vast majority of Christians prefer to think of Christ as God or superman, because this permits them to avoid the imperative of imitation. They know they are not divine or superhuman, and so do not need to consider sacrificing themselves for love just because Christ did. It takes an extremely conscious and deliberate effort to take seriously those moments in the life of Christ when his humanity is most manifest. That he was born and died, ate and drank, and walked the earth is no problem. There is nothing distinctively human about these activities. What is truly human is to struggle to discern one's vocation, to shape one's destiny in the face of adversity, to confront violent death. By putting Jesus in parallel with Paul, who obviously had to make such crucial and fundamental choices, we are forced to recognize that Jesus went through the same agonizing process.

Bibliography

Asher, Jeffrey R. *Polarity and Change in 1 Corinthians 15. A Study of Metaphysics, Rhetoric and Resurrection.* Tübingen: Mohr Siebeck, 2000.

Barr, James. "Abba Isn't 'Daddy.'" *Journal of Theological Studies* 39 (1988) 28–47.

Barrett, C. K. *A Commentary on the Second Epistle to the Corinthians.* Harper's NT Commentaries. New York: Harper, 1973.

Bartchy, S. Scott. "Slavery." *Anchor Bible Dictionary.* New York: Doubleday, 1992, 6:65–73.

Boll, F. "Die Lebensalter." *Neue Jarbücher für das Klassische Altertum* 31 (1913) 89–145.

Boslooper, Thomas. *The Virgin Birth.* London: SCM Press, 1962.

Brown, Raymond E. "The Problem of the Virginal Conception of Jesus." *Theological Studies* 33 (1972) 3–34.

———. *The Birth of the Messiah. A Commentary on the Infancy Narratives in Matthew and Luke.* New Updated Edition. New York: Doubleday, 1993.

———. *The Death of the Messiah. From Gethsemane to the Grave.* Anchor Bible Reference Library. New York: Doubleday, 1994.

Brown, Raymond E., and others. *Mary in the New Testament. A Collaborative Assessment by Protestant and Roman Catholic Scholars.* Philadelphia: Fortress/New York: Paulist, 1978.

Bruce, F. F. *Philippians.* New International Bible Commentary. Peabody, MA: Hendrickson, 1989.

Casson, Lionel. *Libraries in the Ancient World.* New Haven, CT: Yale University Press, 2002.

Collins, John. *The Scepter and the Star. The Messiahs of the Dead Sea Scrolls and Other Ancient Literature.* Anchor Bible Reference Library. New York: Doubleday, 1995.

Danby, Herbert. *The Mishnah.* Oxford: Oxford University Press, 1933.

Daube, David. "The Earliest Structure of the Gospels." *New Testament Studies* 5 (1958–1959) 174–87.

Davies, W. D. *Torah in the Messianic Age and/or the Age to Come.* Journal of Biblical Literature Monograph Series, 7. Philadelphia: Society of Biblical Literature, 1952.

Davies, W. D., and Dale Allison. *A Critical and Exegetical Commentary on the Gospel of Matthew.* I. *Chs. 1–7.* International Critical Commentary. Edinburgh: Clark, 1988.

———. *A Critical and Exegetical Commentary on the Gospel of Matthew.* II. *Chs. 8–18.* International Critical Commentary. Edinburgh: Clark, 1991.

Dodd, C. H. *Historical Tradition in the Fourth Gospel.* Cambridge: Cambridge University Press, 1963.

Dunn, James D. G. *Christology in the Making. An Inquiry into the Origins of the Doctrine of the Incarnation.* London: SCM Press, 1980.

———. *The Theology of Paul the Apostle.* Grand Rapids, MI: Eerdmans, 1998.

———. *Christianity in the Making.* I. *Jesus Remembered.* Grand Rapids, MI: Eerdmans, 2003.

Finkelstein, L. "The Oldest Midrash: Pre-Rabbinic Ideals and Teaching in the Passover Haggadah." *Harvard Theological Review* 31 (1938) 291–317.

Fitzmyer, Joseph A. *The Gospel according to Luke (I–IX).* New York: Doubleday, 1981.

———. *The Gospel according to Luke (X–XXIV).* New York: Doubleday, 1985.

Freyne, Sean. *Galilee, Jesus and the Gospels. Literary Approaches and Historical Investigations.* Dublin: Gill and Macmillan, 1988.

Glancy, Jennifer. *Slavery in Early Christianity.* Oxford: Oxford University Press, 2002.

Hamel, Gildas. *Poverty and Charity in Roman Palestine, First Three Centuries C.E.* Near Eastern Studies 23. Berkeley: University of California Press, 1990.

Hayward, Robert. *The Targum of Jeremiah.* The Aramaic Bible. Vol. 12. Wilmington, DE: Michael Glazier, 1986.

Hedrick, Charles. "Paul's Conversion/Call: A Comparative Analysis of the Three Reports in Acts." *Journal of Biblical Literature* 100 (1981) 415–32.

Hengel, Martin. *Judaism and Hellenism. Studies in Their Encounter in Palestine in the Early Hellenistic Period.* Philadelphia: Fortress Press, 1974.

———. *The Charismatic Leader and His Followers.* Edinburgh: Clark, 1981.

Hoehner, Harold. *Herod Antipas.* Grand Rapids, MI: Zondervan, 1972.

Jeremias, Joachim. *Jerusalem in the Time of Jesus. An Investigation into Economic and Social Conditions during the New Testament Period.* London: SCM Press, 1969.

———. *New Testament Theology.* I, *The Proclamation of Jesus.* London: SCM Press, 1971.

Kelly, J.N.D. *Jerome. His Life, Writings, and Controversies.* London: Duckworth, 1975.

Kim, Seyoon. *The Origin of Paul's Gospel.* Second edition. Tübingen: Mohr Siebeck, 1984.

Luz, Ulrich. *Das Evangelium nach Matthäus.* 1 Teilband. Mt 1–7. Evangelish-katholischer Kommentar zum Neuen Testament 1/1. Zurich: Benziger/Neu-kirchen: Neukirchener Verlag, 1985.

——. *Das Evangelium nach Matthäus.* 2 Teilband. Mt 8–17. Evangelish-katholischer Kommentar zum Neuen Testament 1/2. Zurich: Benziger/Neu-kirchen: Neukirchener Verlag, 1990.

Marrou, H.-I. *Histoire de l'éducation dans l'antiquité.* Paris: Seuil, 1948.

Martin, Dale. *Slavery as Salvation: The Metaphor of Slavery in Pauline Christianity.* New Haven, CT: Yale University Press, 1990.

Martyn, J. Louis. *Theological Issues in the Letters of Paul.* Edinburgh: Clark, 1997a.

——. *Galatians.* Anchor Bible. New York: Doubleday, 1997b.

Meier, John P. *A Marginal Jew. Rethinking the Historical Jesus.* I. *The Roots of the Problem and the Person.* New York: Doubleday, 1991.

——. *A Marginal Jew. Rethinking the Historical Jesus.* II. *Mentor, Message and Miracles.* New York: Doubleday, 1994.

——. *A Marginal Jew. Rethinking the Historical Jesus.* III. *Companions and Competitors.* New York: Doubleday, 2001.

Murphy-O'Connor, Jerome. "John the Baptist and Jesus: History and Hypotheses." *New Testament Studies* 36 (1990) 359–74.

——. "Prisca and Aquila. Travelling Tent-Makers and Church-Builders." *Bible Review* 8/6 (1992) 40–51.

——. "Paul in Arabia." *Catholic Biblical Quarterly* 55 (1993) 732–37.

——. *Paul. A Critical Life.* Oxford: Clarendon Press, 1996.

——. "Jesus and the Money Changers (Mark 11:15-17; John 2:13-17)." *Revue Biblique* 107 (2000) 42-55.

Nolland, John. *Luke 1–9:20.* Dallas: Word Books, 1989.

Oakman, Douglas E. *Jesus and the Economic Questions of His Day.* Studies in the Bible and Early Christianity 8. Lewiston, NY: Mellen Press, 1986.

Perrin, Bernadotte. *Plutarch's Lives.* IX *Demetrius and Antony.* Loeb Classical Library. London: Heinemann, 1920.

Perrin, Norman. *Rediscovering the Teaching of Jesus.* New York: Harper & Row, 1976.

Richardson, Peter. "Why Turn the Tables? Jesus' Protest in the Temple Precincts." *Society of Biblical Literature 1992 Seminar Papers.* No. 31. Ed. E. H. Lovering. Atlanta: Scholars, 507–23, 1992.

——. *Herod. King of the Jews and Friend of the Romans.* Columbia, SC: University of South Carolina Press, 1996.

Sanders, E. P. *Jesus and Judaism.* Philadelphia: Fortress, 1985.

Saulnier, Christiane. "Hérode Antipas et Jean le Baptiste. Quelques remarques sur les confusions chronologiques de Flavius Josèphe." *Revue Biblique* 91 (1984) 362–76.

Schmeller, Thomas. "Stoics, Stoicism." *Anchor Bible Dictionary.* New York: Doubleday, 1992, 6:210–14.

Schürer, Emil. *The History of the Jewish People in the Age of Jesus Christ (175 BC–AD 135)*. Edinburgh: Clark, 1973–87.

Schwartz, Daniel R. "Pontius Pilate." *Anchor Bible Dictionary*. New York: Doubleday, 1992, 5:395–401.

Sherwin-White A. N. *Roman Society and Roman Law in the New Testament*. Oxford: Clarendon Press, 1963.

Sperber, Alexander. *The Bible in Aramaic*. III. *The Latter Prophets according to Targum Jonathan*. Leiden: Brill, 1962.

Spicq, Ceslas. *Les Épitres Pastorales*. Études Bibliques. Paris: Gabalda, 1969.

Stanley, David. "Paul's Conversion in Acts: Why the Three Accounts?" *Catholic Biblical Quarterly* 15 (1953) 315–38.

Sysling, Harry. *Tehiyyat Ha-Metim. The Resurrection of the Dead in the Palestinian Targums of the Pentateuch and the Parallel Traditions in Classical Rabbinic Literature*. Texte und Studien zum Antiken Judentum 57. Tübingen: Mohr Siebeck, 1996.

Van Iersel, B. "The Finding of Jesus in the Temple. Some Observations on the Original Form of Luke ii 41-51a." *Novum Testamentum* 4 (1960) 161–73.

Waterfield, Robin. *Plutarch, The Greek Lives. A Selection of Nine Greek Lives*. Oxford World's Classics. Oxford: Oxford University Press, 1998.

Wilkinson, John. "L'apport de saint Jérôme à la topographie." *Revue Biblique* 81 (1974) 245–57.

Wroe, Ann. *Pontius Pilate. The Biography of an Invented Man*. New York: Random House, 2000.

Yonge, C. D. *The Works of Philo. Complete and Unabridged*. New Updated Edition. Peabody, MA: Hendrickson, 1993.

Subject Index

Index of Old Testament and Other Jewish Sources

Index of New Testament and Other Christian Sources

Classical Authors Index